MARRIAGE, DIVORCE,
AND REMARRIAGE

*Fresh Help and Hope from the Bible*

Daniel Goepfrich

*Marriage, Divorce, and Remarriage:*
*Fresh Help and Hope from the Bible*
by Daniel Goepfrich

Printed in the United States of America

ISBN  978-1-60477-027-8

www.xulonpress.com

*To Saralynn,*
*The "wife of my youth"*
*With whom I covenanted*
*On February 22, 1997*

# TABLE OF CONTENTS

## PART 3: REMARRIAGE

# INTRODUCTION

*"Why don't you just leave it alone?"*

As we approach this issue of marriage, divorce, and remarriage, I understand that there are few topics that bring up more controversy, more uneasiness, and possibly even more bitterness and bad feeling than this.

The reason for this, in my opinion, is that many Christians have never really studied God's Word on the subject, and, therefore, have never made personal, thought-through beliefs. The teaching that is done on these types of issues is usually the result of less true study and more tradition. "This is the way I've always been taught" or "This is what most *[insert your denomination here]* believe" prefaces the teaching. Understandably, most pastors have so many other responsibilities that approaching an issue of this magnitude is overwhelming. Sadly, then, their application is woefully inadequate, and those people involved do not receive the full benefit of God's Word on the matter.

Building upon the tradition problem, those passages which *are* considered are done so with a bias toward one's past teaching. Though this cannot be considered true *study*, it is also not abnormal and should be expected. Let me give an example. I never do the final proofread on any of my writing, because my mind knows what it expects to see. Many others, however, reading for the first time, will catch things that I do not. I read with a bias toward what I meant, rather than what my fingers actually typed.

The same holds true on this issue of biblical marriage, divorce, and remarriage. We tend to look at the same Bible passages with the same bias toward what we *think* those passages teach, instead of reading the words on the page, comparing them to the rest of Scripture, and seeing if there might be another viewpoint which would be worth considering.

Because I believe in the absolute and supreme authority of the Word of God, all the way down to the very words the writers put down, this study will attempt to take a "fresh" look at what the Bible says about marriage, divorce, and remarriage. This is not to say that the ideas and conclusions presented here have never before been offered, because they have been, and by Bible scholars better than I. However, it will be fresh compared to the "accepted" doctrine which supports the many unwritten rules in our churches today.

Unfortunately, this comes too late for many who have been down this brutal path. I heartily agree with Chuck Swindoll who said it well:

> It's time some of us in the evangelical camp came up front and addressed the issue boldly. Many a divorced person is grinding out his or her life under an enormous load of unnecessary guilt. While I certainly would not desire to soften the penetrating blows of the Spirit of God (if, in fact, it *is* the Spirit producing conviction), I do hope that my words provide the breathing room God has allowed in certain instances.[1] (italics original)

Too many people have known the heart-sinking feeling when they hear their pastor's words: "I'm sorry. I can't marry you – you've

---

[1] Charles Swindoll, *Divorce: When It All Comes Tumbling Down* (Portland: Multnomah, 1981), p. 5.

been divorced. You'll have to see the Justice of the Peace (or another minister, etc.)." Sadly, these may have been the same pastors who ("unofficially", of course) recommended that the couple divorce in the first place. And finally, to top it off, once the couple is married – outside of the church – the pastor welcomes them back into the assembly to sit and tithe. They can't serve in any "real" ministry; after all, they have been divorced! All the while, the hurting couple doesn't feel comfortable in any Sunday School class or small group because they "don't fit in". Soon they just stop attending altogether. The heartache is not worth it. Hopefully, they pray, God will forgive them when it comes to Judgment Day. May God have mercy on those who have misused their positions as God's spokesmen and hurt His children!

Why can't we just leave it alone? Henry Morris answers it well:

> The blessings and joys of a true Christian home are worth all the study and

prayers and effort that can be expended
to attain such a home.[2]

---

[2] Henry M. Morris, *The Genesis Record* (Grand Rapids: Baker, 1976), p. 103.

# PART ONE

# MARRIAGE

# CHAPTER ONE
# WHAT IS MARRIAGE?

Some may be thinking, "Why waste time with such a question? Everyone knows what marriage is. Let's get to the good stuff – what does the Bible say about divorce and remarriage?" To these I have to say that it is a false assumption to believe that marriage is too trivial to address first. On the contrary, how can we approach divorce – the dissolution of marriage – or remarriage without first considering the marriage itself. Additionally, it is very obvious to me that many people do not truly understand marriage and all that it entails. That said, let us consider this seemingly basic question: what is marriage?

It seems like we should easily find an answer simply by looking in any dictionary. According to the first entry on Dictionary.com, "marriage" is

> the social institution under which man
> and woman establish their decision to
> live as husband and wife by legal com-
> mitments, religious ceremonies, etc.[1]

Of course, we all know that in order to be married, a couple stands before a minister or judge with a couple of witnesses looking on. After exchanging some vows and (maybe) rings, the official says the magic words, "I now pronounce you husband and wife", and – voilà – they're married!

## The Social Institution

Without even noticing it, you may have completely missed the mistake in that definition above. While it is only one wrong word, this mindset verbalizes the underlying problem of all marriages today and the cause of all divorces. The word? *Social.* The dictionary puts into print the attitude that permeates humanity and is put into action day after day

---

[1] marriage. Dictionary.com. *Dictionary.com Unabridged (v 1.1)*. Random House, Inc.
http://dictionary.reference.com/browse/marriage
(accessed: July 9, 2007).

in the way people approach their current, ex-, and future spouses: marriage is a "social institution."

Big deal, you say. Marriage *is* a social institution. It is recorded and legalized by the state. In fact, marriage can be a great asset in society and the business world – taxes, insurance, social memberships. What is the point?

The same dictionary that gave us the definition above tells us that an "institution" is

> a well-established and structured pattern of behavior or of relationships that is accepted as a fundamental part of a culture, as marriage; *the act of instituting or setting up*, establishment [italics added][2]

Saying that marriage is a social institution is the same as saying that society set up or established marriage. Is this true?

Fortunately we have a record of the very first marriage. Let's consider it for a moment and see just how *society* established this thing called "marriage".

> [18]**Then the LORD God** *said, "It is not good for the man to be alone; I will make him a*

---

[2] institution. Dictionary.com. (accessed: July 09, 2007).

*helper suitable for him."* [19]*Out of the ground* **the LORD God** *formed every beast of the field and every bird of the sky, and brought them to the man to see what he would call them; and whatever the man called a living creature, that was its name.* [20]*The man gave names to all the cattle, and to the birds of the sky, and to every beast of the field, but for Adam there was not found a helper suitable for him.* [21]**So the LORD God** *caused a deep sleep to fall upon the man, and he slept; then He took one of his ribs and closed up the flesh at that place.* [22]**The LORD God** *fashioned into a woman the rib which He had taken from the man, and brought her to the man.*

Genesis 2:18-22

In this passage, I find no society at all. I see only one person on the planet until the wedding day. I see no engagement, no physical checkup, no marriage license, or recorder's office. In fact, I see God initiating the whole thing: "It is not good... [therefore] I will make." So let me ask: is marriage a social institution or is it, actually, a divine institution?

If this seems to you to be a game of semantics, you have not grasped the importance of the matter. I said earlier that the word "social" reflects the attitude that mankind as a whole expresses toward marriage. If society established marriage, if it was mankind who set up this whole concept, then society has the absolute right and prerogative to decide the ground rules surrounding marriage, including its permanence or dissolution, the number and gender of its participants, and much more.

But society did *not* establish it. Man did *not* initiate marriage. *God did!* And if marriage was God's idea, started by God, then all of those rules can and must be decided and enforced by God alone. This is not a word game; this is the basis for everything that we know and must believe about marriage. Until we understand that God is the only One from Whom we should get our information about marriage, our marriages are in trouble and will not survive the demonic attacks that meet them every day – the divorce, the abuse, the neglect, the homosexuality, the partner-swapping, and all the rest. Jesus underscored this fact when He made the oft-quoted statement, "What therefore *God has joined together*, let no man separate." (Mark 10:9, italics added)

> Marriage is not an invention of men, but a divine institution, and therefore is to be religiously observed, and the more, because it is a figure of the mystical in-

7

separable union between Christ and his church.[3]

In Genesis 2:18-22, God instituted marriage and established the basis for it. Notice the elements involved in God's pattern:

First, *marriage was to remove Adam's loneliness.* We will discuss this topic further in the next chapter.

Secondly, *there was one man, Adam, and one woman, Eve* (see Genesis 3:20). This marriage was neither homosexual nor polygamous. It was not Adam and Steve. Neither was it Adam and Eve...and Rachel...and Miriam...and Ruth, etc. In fact, when Jesus and Paul quoted this passage, they both specifically noted that "the *two* shall become one flesh" (italics added; see Matthew 19:5; Mark 10:8; 1 Corinthians 6:16).

Finally, *God brought the man and woman together.* In the case of Adam and Eve, this was done literally: He walked Eve to Adam's side. The principle, however, still applies today – God brings people together for marriage.

---

[3] Matthew Henry, *Commentary on the Whole Bible* (Peabody, MA: Hendrickson, 1991) p. 1799.

Marriages (they say) are made in heaven: we are sure this one was, for the man, the woman, the match, were all God's own work.[4]

## Of Leaving and Cleaving

*For this reason a man shall leave his father and his mother, and be joined ["cleave", KJV] to his wife; and they shall become one flesh.*

Genesis 2:24

The words "leave" (Hebrew `azab – "leave, forsake, loose"[5]) and "be joined" (Hebrew *dabaq* – "cling, cleave, keep close"[6]) are both action verbs that are to be initiated by the man. He is the one who leaves his father and mother, and he is the one who joins himself to his wife. She does not initiate the joining together. While this is not to say that the woman should *not* leave her family and join

---

[4] Henry, p. 10.

[5] Francis Brown, S. R. Driver, Charles A. Briggs, *The New Brown-Driver-Briggs-Gesenius Hebrew and English Lexicon* (electronic edition). (Hereafter cited as BDB.)

[6] *Ibid.*, p. 179.

9

her husband, the principle is that it is the man's responsibility, as the head of the newly formed household, to initiate the changes as they begin their new life together.

In the New Testament passages dealing with cleaving, we find that this "joining together" is more than just living together (as common law marriage suggests) or even sexual intercourse. In Romans 7:2, Paul refers to a married woman as "bound by law to her [living] husband" and "released from the law concerning" him at his death. Further, in 1 Corinthians 7 he uses the terms "bondage" (vs. 15), and again "bound" and "released" (vs. 27). There is a far deeper than physical connection that happens at the joining of two people in marriage. We will discuss this more in the next chapter.

> See here how great the virtue of a divine ordinance is; the bonds of it are stronger even than those of nature. To whom can we be more firmly bound than the father that begat us and the mothers that bore us? Yet the son must quit them, to be joined to his wife, and the daughter forget them, to cleave to her husband, Ps. 45:10, 11.[7]

---

[7] *Ibid.*

In his excellent little book, *I Married You*, Walter Trobisch indicates that Genesis 2:24 contains the three elements necessary for a truly Biblical marriage. There must be a "leaving", a "cleaving" and a fusion into "one flesh." Unless all three of these take place, there is no true marriage between the two people involved.[8]

---

[8] Cleveland McDonald, *God's Plan for Family Living* (Schaumburg, IL: Regular Baptist Press, 1977), p. 9.

# CHAPTER TWO
# WHY MARRIAGE?

We have already seen that it was not society who instituted marriage, but rather God. The next question that begs to be asked and answered is, "Why?" Why did God institute a one man / one woman joining as He did? There is no marriage among the angels (see Matthew 22:30; Mark 12:25). Why are we not like them?

## Not Good

On the sixth day of God's creative masterpiece, God made the first human beings.

> *26Then God said, "Let Us make man in Our image, according to Our likeness; and let them rule over the fish of the sea and over the birds of the sky and over the cattle and over all the earth, and over every creeping thing that creeps on the earth." 27God created man in His own image, in the image*

> *of God He created him; male and female He*
> *created them.*

> Genesis 1:26-27

It sounds simple enough, to be sure. As He was finishing up the creation that He had begun earlier in the week, He made a man and a woman. It isn't until we get to the end of the next chapter, however, that Moses fills us in on the details of this unique creative work. Let's look again at this passage:

> [18]*Then the LORD God said, "It is not good for the man to be alone; I will make him a helper suitable for him."* [19]*Out of the ground the LORD God formed every beast of the field and every bird of the sky, and brought them to the man to see what he would call them; and whatever the man called a living creature, that was its name.* [20]*The man gave names to all the cattle, and to the birds of the sky, and to every beast of the field, but for Adam there was not found a helper suitable for him.* [21]*So the LORD God caused a deep sleep to fall upon the man, and he slept; then He took one of his ribs and closed up the flesh at that place.* [22]*The LORD God fashioned into a woman the rib which He had taken from the man, and brought her to the man.*

> Genesis 2:18-22

Previously that day, God had made the "living creatures...creeping things and beasts of the earth" (Genesis 1:24), then He created Adam, the first human. However, there was a problem: Adam was alone.

A glance back to our dictionary tells us that to be *lonely* is to be "destitute of sympathetic or friendly companionship."[1] Unlike the angels, Adam was created "in the image of God" (Genesis 1:27). This does not mean that Adam was created in God's *physical* image, because "God is a spirit" (John 4:24) and does not have a body which He could copy. However, there are some parts of God that could be used as a pattern for Adam: emotion, intellect, will, authority, morality, and much more. When God created Adam in His own image, He bestowed upon him His very *nature*. For Adam, that included being a social being as God is. Adam needed companionship. God looked at His creation and said that it was "not good", it was still incomplete, because Adam was still incomplete: he had no companion.

But Adam did not know this. He looked finished. He felt complete. He was unaware that something was lacking, so God showed him. To Adam God brought the various kinds of animals, "every beast of the

---

[1] lonely. Dictionary.com. (accessed: July 09, 2007).

field and every bird of the sky…to see what he would call them" (Genesis 2:19). See, God isn't stupid, and neither was Adam. God knew that as Adam watched these animals prancing past him, he would begin to notice a pattern: there was always a pair, like a matched set, of each of the animals. God knew that it would not be long before Adam began to wonder, "Do I have a match? Where is the other one like me?" But there was none to be found. He was *alone.*

> In all the animal kingdom, there could not be found a "helper like him." [Adam] alone, of all creatures, was really alone. And that was not good! Before God could declare His creation "finished" and "very good," this all-important deficiency must be eliminated. God would provide such a helper and companion for Adam, one "like" him, and yet different, perfectly complementing him and completing God's work.[2]

## The Covenant of Companionship

This subtitle was coined by Dr. Jay Adams in his classic work on this subject, and

---

[2] Morris, p. 98.

we would do well to examine his points here. To understand his premise, read these two passages and the following paragraphs where he explains his conclusion.

> *[The adulteress] leaves the **companion** of her youth and forgets the **covenant** of her God;*

> Proverbs 2:17

> *Yet you say, 'For what reason?' Because the LORD has been a witness between you and the wife of your youth, against whom you have dealt treacherously, though she is your **companion** and your wife by **covenant**.*

> Malachi 2:14

Now we must consider in detail what we have already seen to be the very essence of marriage: *companionship.* God made most of us so that we would be lonely without an intimate companion with whom to live. God provided Eve not only (or even primarily) as Adam's helper (though help is also one dimension of companionship), but as his companion. He too, as all other husbands since (we shall see), is to provide companionship for her.

Turning once more to Proverbs 2:17 and Malachi 2:14 (not to mention Ezek. 16:8, 9 to which I referred earlier), note that forsaking the companion of one's youth is paralleled with forgetting the covenant of God (Prov. 2:17)...Forsaking a companion is the same as forgetting the marriage covenant.

In Malachi 2:14, a similar concept emerges. There, God denounces husbands who are faithless to their companions. These companions are further described as those who are wives by covenant (NASB). So, in both passages where companionship is prominently mentioned, so is the covenantal aspect of marriage. That means that (as I have pointed out) marriage is a *Covenant of Companionship*.[3] [all italics original]

It is not enough for us to have a sexual partner with whom we share our lives. We have already seen that loneliness, being without companionship, is "not good" in light of God's purpose for most people.[4] However, as

---

[3] Jay E. Adams, *Marriage, Divorce, and Remarriage in the Bible* (Grand Rapids: Zondervan, 1980), pp. 11, 15.

[4] Paul's teaching on the benefits for some people to remain single is well beyond the scope of this immediate study. The blessedness of being single in Christ will have to be approached at another time. See 1 Corinthians 7:25-40 for Paul on this subject.

we have already mentioned with the "joining" together in marriage, there is a far deeper than physical connection that happens at the joining of two people in marriage.

Marriage was divinely established for God's people. At the beginning of time, when God brought Adam and Eve together, they knew nothing about sin and had no thought that anything would change their relationship with God. However, when sin *did* break that relationship (see Genesis 3), all of mankind became spiritually separated from God (Romans 5:12; Ephesians 2:1). While I will not go so far to say that God does not recognize marriages between people who have never accepted Jesus' forgiveness and salvation, marriage is still God's institution, and their marriage vows are made before a God with whom they do not have a relationship.

God's children, on the other hand – those who know Jesus personally in their lives – are in an altogether different situation. God says that they vows they make *to* each other are actually covenants *with* each other, with God standing as a witness. These covenants, or spiritual contracts, are lasting until one of the partners dies, whether or not the words "until death do us part" are specified. To God, that phrase is not optional. The marriage covenant between Christians before God, solemnized by vows, is a lifetime agreement.[5]

> The woman was created, not of dust of the earth, but from a rib of Adam, because she was formed for an inseparable unity and fellowship of life with the man, and the mode of her creation was to lay the actual foundation for the moral ordinance of marriage.[6]

To reinforce this concept, Paul uses poignant phrasing in Romans 7:1-3:

> [1]*Or do you not know, brethren (for I am speaking to those who know the law), that the law has jurisdiction over a person as long as he lives?* [2]*For **the married woman is bound by law to her husband** while he is living; but if her husband dies, **she is released from the law** concerning the hus-*

---

[5] Too many modern marriage "vows" are not really even vows at all. Many consist of nothing more than "I love you because you make me laugh and we like the same flavor of coffee." These are not binding vows. These are simply expressions of current feelings. If that is all that the marriage is based upon, it is no wonder that the slightest thing is grounds for divorce!

[6] C. F. Keil, F. Delitzsch, *Commentary on the Old Testament* (Grand Rapids: Eerdmans, 1980), vol.1, p. 89. (Hereafter cited as K&D.)

> band. ³*So then, if while her husband is liv-*
> *ing she is joined to another man, she shall be*
> *called an adulteress; but **if her husband***
> ***dies, she is free from the law**, so that she*
> *is not an adulteress though she is joined to*
> *another man.*

The Greek root word translated "bound" in verse two (*deō* – "to confine a person or thing by various kinds of restraints; to constrain by law and duty; bind, tie"[7]) gives us an understanding of three common references to marriage. Newlywed couples are said to have "tied the knot". Many times husbands refer to their wives as "the old ball and chain". As funny (or not) as it may sound, both of these accurately describe the "marriage bond" (another common phrase): an unbreakable unity, or link, between the partners under contract. Until Christians enter marriage with the understanding that they are about to make a covenant with each other, one where death is the only "release", no matter the circums-

---

[7] Frederick William Danker, ed., Walter Bauer, W. F. Arndt, F. W. Gingrich, *A Greek-English Lexicon of the New Testament and other Early Christian Literature* (electronic edition). (Hereafter cited as BDAG).

tances, we will continue to see the divorce rate inside the church match that outside it.

## Yes, But Practically Speaking...

When Jesus gave his answer to the Pharisees' question on divorce (which we will study in detail in part two), the disciples responded with a thought you may be having right now:

> *The disciples said to Him, "If the relationship of the man with his wife is like this, it is better not to marry."*

> Matthew 19:10

You know what, Jesus? If I am going to be stuck with this person until death, maybe I should really reconsider this marriage thing. After all, how do I know that we are really right for each other without giving it a try first? If that's a no-go, then maybe I just shouldn't marry at all!

*YES!!!* Finally, a glimpse of hope! That is exactly the point that Jesus was trying to make. The marriage vows are much too important to make without considerable prayer, advice, and forethought. God has determined that marriage is permanent, for life. Because of this it is imperative that couples seek the counsel of many (preferably Christian) elders and counselors *before* getting into this contract, getting burnt, and finding out that it's too late to back out.

## How Sweet It Is

I should mention here that as bad as it may seem to have to live by these harsh rules (sarcasm intended), God really does want most people to marry, and He will bless marriages that are entered into and lived out according to His plan. Remember, He was the One Who instituted it in the first place and called it "good". And not only this, but marriage is a wonderful thing in itself.

> *Do we not have a right to take along a believing wife, even as the rest of the apostles and the brothers of the Lord and Cephas?*

> 1 Corinthians 9:5

Each of the apostles had the choice to marry or to abstain from marrying; Paul chose to remain single. Peter, we know, had a wife (Matthew 8:14). Paul's reference to "the rest of the apostles and the brothers of the Lord" seems to indicate that they all may have been married.

23

There are three main principles to glean from this passage in 1 Corinthians 9.[8]  First, *it is acceptable for ministers of the gospel to marry.* Churches and others that forbid certain people to marry contradict the apostles' example and the Word of God (see 1 Timothy 4:1-5).

Secondly, *it is acceptable for missionaries to marry and to take their wives with them wherever they go.*  The apostles were missionaries, and they took their wives.  Couples and families can minister effectively together.

Thirdly, *there are men and women, like Paul, who can do more good and be more effective in God's ministry if they are not married*; this is also acceptable (see Paul's discussion on this in 1 Corinthians 7:32-35).

## Marriage is Honorable

*Marriage is to be held in honor among all, and the marriage bed is to be undefiled; for fornicators and adulterers God will judge.*

Hebrews 13:4

---

[8] Albert Barnes, *Barnes' Notes on the Old and New Testaments* (electronic edition), "1 Corinthians 9:5".

The writer of Hebrews was not simply making a statement but was actually pleading with his readers concerning this issue. In his wonderful expansion of the New Testament, Dr. Kenneth Wuest translates the verse:

> Let your marriage be held in honor in all things, and thus let your marriage-bed be undefiled, for whoremongers and adulterers God will judge.[9]

Notice that it is the married couple who keeps their bed from becoming defiled by honoring their marriage "in all things". A defiled marriage does not happen when the marriage partners are working together, under the guidance of the Holy Spirit of God, to keep it. However, if the couple does not honor this union, many things could happen that should not.

Marriage is honorable because God established it in the perfect environment. Jesus honored marriage by attending a wedding and performing His first miracle there. When partners honor their marriage, they prevent a defiled bed.[10]

---

[9] Kenneth S. Wuest, *Word Studies in the Greek New Testament* (Grand Rapids: Eerdmans, 1992), vol. 4, p. 536.

[10] Henry, p. 2406.

In their magnificent work, *Theological Wordbook of the Old Testament*, the editors sum up very well this institution called marriage:

> [Under God's law] marriage was to be observed both as an act (I Cor 7:2) and as a structural institution (Eph 5:23). It was honorable (Heb 13:4). Mates were to be chosen from the covenant community (Ex 34:16; cf. II Cor 6:14ff.; Heb 11:31; Mt 1:5). Captive women became members of the covenant community by virtue of marriage (Deut 21:13). Polygamy, implicitly forbidden in the creation covenant, was probably forbidden in Lev 18:18. Marriage was covenantly constituted before God (Prov 2:17), required the husband's evidenced ability to support a family (Prov 24:27), and love for his wife (Prov 5:15-19; cf. Eph 5:25)[11]

## Concluding Thought

It is striking to note that the strength of marriage lies in the faithfulness of the marriage partners – faithfulness to their marriage vows; faithfulness to each other and their marriage bed in sexual purity; and faithfulness to the

---

[11] R. Laird Harris, Gleason L. Archer, Jr., Bruce K. Waltke, *Theological Wordbook of the Old Testament* (Chicago: Moody, 1980), vol.2, "1273", p. 543. (Hereafter cited as *TWOT*.)

God who instituted marriage in the first place. If faithfulness in one or more of these is lacking, the marriage union will not be strong and will probably not last.

The last one is especially important because when two people are married who do not have the proper relationship to God, their marriage is being held together by nothing but the first two: promises and sex! What happens when one partner "doesn't love" the other anymore? What happens when the sex is no longer as it once was? How can a marriage survive the tough times? It *can't* without God! Each of the partners must have a relationship with Jesus Christ, repenting of his or her personal sin and unbelief, and allowing God to control his or her life. At that point the marriage rests in God's hands, His control. No matter the circumstances, good or bad, the marriage bond can hold.

# CHAPTER THREE
## MARITAL RESPONSIBILITIES

As we finish this part dealing with biblical marriage, it seems fitting to take a brief look at some of the responsibilities involved in this divine institution. As we have seen previously, since marriage originated from God, it is God from whom we must get the ground rules regarding marriage. So let us return to His Word and see what responsibilities God expects and intends each partner to fulfill. While this is not an exhaustive list, it gives a good basis for your own personal study of your responsibilities in your marriage.[1] Let's talk about the husbands first.

---

[1] These responsibilities are not necessarily listed in their order of importance. "First", "second", etc. are simply indications of how they are covered in this chapter rather than how God orders them.

## Responsibilities of the Husband

First, *the husband is to be the head of his family.*

> For the husband is the head of the wife, as
> Christ also is the head of the church, He
> Himself being the Savior of the body.

Ephesians 5:23

Too many times those of us who hold to this teaching have been criticized because we are misunderstood to mean that a husband is more important than his wife. This cannot be further from the truth! Being the head of something is not the same as being the most important or even more important than others. Is a CEO more important than the employees? Is a pastor more important than the church members? Consider 1 Corinthians 11:3:

> But I want you to understand that Christ is
> the head of every man, and the man is the
> head of a woman, and **God is the head of
> Christ.**

To say that a husband being the head of his wife means that he is more important than she is the same as saying that God the Father is more important than Jesus Christ because Paul called Him "the head of Christ." How absurd! We know that God the Father and Jesus are equals in the Godhead; they simply have different *functions*. The Christian marriage is the same. The husband and wife are both equally important; they simply have different functions. These functions, or responsibilities, are what we are discussing now.

Secondly, *the husband is to love his wife.*

> 25*Husbands, love your wives, just as Christ also loved the church and gave Himself up for her...* 28*So husbands ought also to love their own wives as their own bodies. He who loves his own wife loves himself...* 33*Nevertheless, each individual among you also is to love his own wife even as himself, and the wife must see to it that she respects her husband.*

> Ephesians 5:25, 28, 33

"Too easy! Didn't I pledge my love to her at our wedding? Of course I love her. How foolish to even have to mention it." Humanly speaking, it seems odd that God would specifically command husbands to love their wives. If love were a natural part of marriage, as most seem to think, why would He waste His inspiration on something so trivial?

The problem is that what *we* associate with love is not *God's* idea of perfect love. For many husbands, even Christian husbands, "loving" their wives consists of giving her kisses (chocolate or otherwise), notes, and gifts. Getting her a glass of water while I'm already in the kitchen is a sure sign of love, isn't it?

While these things are all fine, they don't add up to the love of Ephesians 5. Husbands are told to love their wives *"just as Christ also loved the church"*. And how was that? Continue reading: He *"gave Himself up for her"*. God's love is a love that sacrifices everything necessary for the benefit of the object of its love because of the value placed on the object of the love by the lover. For Christ, that meant sacrificing His very life for the Church, the object of His love. For a husband, the object of his love is his wife. Husbands are commanded to make sacrifices for their wives. Yes, this sometimes includes letting her pick the Friday night movie rental when you really want a different one. But usually it means something much greater. Every family and family situation is different. This is why God's guidance is imperative in marital decisions. Each husband should be in tune with God on what sacrifices are necessary for his immediate marital situation.

Thirdly, *the husband is to be involved in child-rearing.*

> Fathers, do not provoke your children to anger, but bring them up in the discipline and instruction of the Lord.

Ephesians 6:4

I say "be involved in child-rearing" because too often husbands leave all of that to "the woman". While I believe that to be one extreme, I see the other extreme when I hear mothers say to their children, "Just wait until your father gets home!" As in most cases, both extremes should be avoided. It is neither the father's nor the mother's job to rear the children; it is the *parents'* job.

While this is not a book on child-rearing, allow me to make a note here. Just as adults have different personalities and learning styles, so do children. I think Solomon hinted at this in Proverbs 22:6 when he wrote, *"Train up a child in the way he should go, even when he is old he will not depart from it."* The way one child should go (or be taught) is not necessarily the way the others should go (or be taught). Parents, be careful to train each of your children in the way that is best for him or her. This

33

requires a good relationship with each one to discover what that best way is.

Finally, *the husband is to provide for his family.*

> But if anyone does not provide for his own, and especially for those of his household, he has denied the faith and is worse than an unbeliever.

1 Timothy 5:8

It seems like not much would need to be said about this beyond what Paul told Timothy. Not providing for one's household is identified with denying the faith. It is obvious that this is important to God, and we husbands dare not miss it.

However, the question arises, "What exactly does it mean to 'provide'?" Is it true, what we are often taught, that the husband is required to work outside of the home, "providing" a paycheck to pay the bills and buy the groceries? What about a situation where the wife (who *must* work because the husband's sole income has never been enough) has received pay increases, raising her salary well above that of her husband. Together they decide that, since his income is now paying

34

only for childcare, it may be best at the current time for him to stay home with the children, thus eliminating the childcare costs and still being involved in their rearing. Does this count as "providing for his own"?

In his excellent comments on the Greek New Testament, Kenneth Wuest gives us some useful information regarding the word translated "provide".

> The word "provide" is *pronoeō*, "to perceive before, foresee, think of beforehand, provide, to take thought for, care for." Vincent says that "the A.V., uses *provide* in its earlier and more literal meaning of *taking thought in advance...*"

> The words, "his own," refer to near relatives, "of his own house," to members of one's own household.

> Translation. *But if, as is the case, a certain one does not* **anticipate the needs of his own and provide for them,** *and especially for those of his own household, he had denied the Faith and is worse than an unbeliever.*[2] [italics all original, emphasis added]

---

[2] Wuest, vol. 2, p. 81.

We have welcomed Albert Barnes' comments on other passages, and I think that he makes some particularly insightful points on this verse as well.

> The meaning is, that the person referred to is to think beforehand (*pronoei*) of the probable needs of his own family, and make arrangements to meet them. God thus provides for our needs; that is, he sees beforehand what we shall need, and makes arrangements for those needs by long preparation. The food that we eat, and the raiment that we wear, he foresaw that we should need, and the arrangement for the supply was made years since, and to meet these needs he has been carrying forward the plans of his providence in the seasons; in the growth of animals; in the formation of fruit; in the bountiful harvest. So, according to our measure, we are to anticipate what will be the probable needs of our families, and to make arrangements to meet them. The words "his own," refer to those who are naturally dependent on him, whether living in his own immediate family or not. There may be many distant relatives naturally dependent on our aid, besides those who live in our own house.[3]

---

[3] Barnes, "1 Timothy 5:8".

So it is reasonable enough to say that if God has blessed the wife's endeavors (we will later consider passages about her working) to help her husband in his provision – forethought and planning regarding the family needs – there is no absolute command that she not work away from the home.[4] Naturally, if one is able to not work outside the home, neither he nor she, as the case may be, should "watch soap operas and eat bonbons" all day.[5] Paul makes it very clear that *"if anyone is not willing to work, then he is not to eat, either"* (2 Thessalonians 3:10). As any homemaker will testify, there is plenty of work to do in the home as well.

---

[4] However, as we will note later in the wife's responsibilities, this is not the intended standard set up by God. His intention is that the man is indeed working as the primary "breadwinner" of the home. This is still seen in the natural order of things. Consider a potential employer's initial response when the answer to his question, "What is this gap in your résumé?" is answered by, "Well, I stayed at home with the kids while my wife worked." Though the reason may be perfectly valid, it will still typically receive a negative response.

[5] My mother's favorite response when someone calls her at work (outside the home, by the way) and asks what she is doing is, "Oh, just watching soap operas and eating bonbons. *Ha!*"

## Responsibilities of the Wife

In discussing the responsibilities related to the husbands, we found that husbands are to take the leadership role, being the head of the wife and family. Being the leader, sacrificing for his wife, providing for the family, rearing the children – at times this can put tremendous pressure on the husband. What, if anything, is the wife to do about all of this? Let's see!

First, *the wife is to be her husband's helper*.

> *18Then the LORD God said, "It is not good for the man to be alone; I will make him a helper suitable for him."...21So the LORD God caused a deep sleep to fall upon the man, and he slept; then He took one of his ribs and closed up the flesh at that place. 22The LORD God fashioned into a woman the rib which He had taken from the man, and brought her to the man.*

> Genesis 2:18, 21-22

I think it's important that the second chapter of the Bible, while discussing the institution of marriage, contains the very first responsibility that *a wife is to be her husband's helper*. In the last chapter we discussed the role of companionship in the marriage, so it is unnecessary to repeat it all here. However, let

38

me re-emphasize its importance. Wives, you were created primarily for the purpose of being your husband's companion. This includes being his helper. Remember that when God brings two people together, He brings people who are comparable, suitable, for each other. If God brought you and your husband together, then you *are* suitable to help him (no matter what you may think at times). This is God's desire for you, that you be a help, not a hindrance, to your husband.

Secondly, *the wife is to be subject to and respect her husband.*

> [22]*Wives, be subject to your own husbands, as to the Lord.* [23]*For the husband is the head of the wife, as Christ also is the head of the church, He Himself being the Savior of the body.* [24]*But as the church is subject to Christ, so also the wives ought to be to their husbands in everything...*[33]*Nevertheless, each individual among you also is to love his own wife even as himself, and the wife must see to it that she respects her husband.*

> Ephesians 5:22-24, 33

This responsibility given by God to wives is probably the most hotly contested. In our modern "I have my rights" society, many women have been brainwashed into believing that "being subject" or "submitting" to their husbands means to be inferior to them. While we have already touched on this above regarding the husband being the head of the household, we would do well to take another look because the truth here cannot be emphasized too strongly. *A wife is not inferior to her husband in the bond of marriage!* Anyone who teaches otherwise is not using the Bible as his (or her) guide. Anyone who thinks that the Bible teaches this misunderstands and is greatly deceived. The Bible makes it very clear that in biblical marriage the wife is her husband's *helper*, never his *slave*.

However, as we noted earlier, the wife does have a very different function in marriage than her husband. Just as a leader is not a leader when he has no followers, the husband cannot be the head of the household if no one is subject to him. This is where the wife enters. Let's look at this phrase "be subject" (or "submit yourselves") for a moment.

The Greek word from which we get the translations "be subject" and "submit yourselves" is actually a compound word, *hupotassō*, from two other words: *hupo* – "under" and *tassō* – "arrange, put in place".[6] While "arranging under" does refer to how things are ranked and ordered – one thing subject to (ranked under) another, *hupotassō* is never used in reference to the superiority, inferiority, or importance of the objects or people in question. In fact, except for once, every time that *hupotassō* is used actively in the New Testament (meaning forcing submission upon someone or something else), it is always in reference to Jesus Christ submitting things to Himself.[7] All of the other uses are passive, meaning *voluntary* submission. Here is just one example.

After Joseph and Mary returned to Jerusalem to find Jesus, Luke tells us that He returned to Nazareth with them and "continued in subjection to them" (2:51). "Subjection" here is *hupotassō*, in the passive voice, meaning a voluntary, deliberate obedience to the will of His earthly parents.

---

[6] BDAG, *hupotasso.*

[7] Gerhard Kittel, Gerhard Friedrich, eds., *Theological Dictionary of the New Testament* (Grand Rapids: Eerdmans, 1972), vol.8, p. 41. (Hereafter cited as *TDNT.*)

For example, Hebrews 2:8 – *"For in subjecting all things to him, He left nothing that is not subject to him."* See also 1 Corinthians 15:25-28, Ephesians 1:22, 1 Peter 3:22.

So what does it mean to submit yourself to your husband? Simply this: your husband is the one responsible to God for how he leads the family. You are responsible to God for how you follow his lead. Yes, your husband is the final human authority in your home. He should consider your opinion and advice since you are his suitable companion and helper, but ultimately he must decide how your family goes. Before God, you must follow him.[8] God will hold *you* accountable for how you voluntarily follow your husband's leadership (including your attitude toward him and his leadership), not for what he does with your opinions or suggestions.

Thirdly, *the wife is to take care of the daily operation of the house and family.* Consider these two passages, one from each Testament.

> *Therefore, I want younger widows to get married, <u>bear children</u>, <u>keep house</u>, and give the enemy no occasion for reproach;*
>
> 1 Timothy 5:14

---

[8] In those instances where your husband is in obvious contradiction, or even defiance, to the Word of God, you should consult your local church elders who can help you and your husband through those details which I shall not try to address here.

*10 An excellent wife, who can find? For her worth is far above jewels. 11 The heart of her husband trusts in her, and he will have no lack of gain. 12 She does him good and not evil all the days of her life. 13 She looks for wool and flax and works with her hands in delight. 14 She is like merchant ships; she brings her food from afar. 15 She rises also while it is still night and gives food to her household and portions to her maidens. 16 She considers a field and buys it; from her earnings she plants a vineyard. 17 She girds herself with strength and makes her arms strong. 18 She senses that her gain is good; her lamp does not go out at night. 19 She stretches out her hands to the distaff, and her hands grasp the spindle. 20 She extends her hand to the poor, and she stretches out her hands to the needy. 21 She is not afraid of the snow for her household, for all her household are clothed with scarlet. 22 She makes coverings for herself; her clothing is fine linen and purple. 23 Her husband is known in the gates, when he sits among the elders of the land. 24 She makes linen garments and sells them, and supplies belts to the tradesmen. 25 Strength and dignity are her clothing, and she smiles at the future. 26 She opens her mouth in wisdom, and the teaching of kindness is on her tongue. 27 She looks well to the ways of her household, and does not eat the bread of idleness. 28 Her children rise up and bless her; her husband also, and he praises her, saying: 29 "Many daughters have done nobly, but you excel them all." 30 Charm is deceitful and beauty*

> *is vain, but a woman who fears the LORD,*
> *she shall be praised.* [31] *Give her the product*
> *of her hands, and let her works praise her in*
> *the gates.*

Proverbs 31:10-31

I have taken the liberty of underlining some of the attributes in the above verses which this responsibility involves. Since this portion of Proverbs 31 is sometimes referred to as qualities of "the perfect wife", let's look at her. The "perfect wife":

- is trustworthy (vs. 11)
- sews for and clothes the family (vs. 13, 19, 21-22, 24)
- shops wisely (vs. 14)
- prepares meals (vs. 15)
- is a decision-maker in the home (vs. 16)
- is hospitable (vs. 20)
- teaches (vs. 26)
- manages the household; is not idle (vs. 27)
- bears the children; keeps the house (1 Timothy 5:14)

Does this sound like an inferior nobody? *No!* The wife has many functions to fulfill to keep the house running when the husband is not there (presumably working to provide for his family).

I can see the other side of the feminist argument coming full speed: "I thought the wife wasn't a slave. It sure sounds like it to me." Well, no one said that marriage and making a home was going to be easy. It's not; in fact, it's a lot of work! Remember that marriage is a covenant, an agreement, between a man and a woman, not just to love each other – though that is important – but also to be companions to each other, divinely suited to help each other.

According to God's Word, the man is to be providing for his family (1 Timothy 5:8). Just a couple verses later Paul gives the wife's primary compatibility job: bear children and keep the house. (We have already discussed possible exceptions to this standard.) This does not make her inferior. It's actually just the opposite: the wife is divinely decreed to maintain the home, protecting and teaching their children. To be a homemaker (not "housewife") is the greatest profession to which a woman could ever be called. Women, don't let yourselves be deceived by those who contradict God's Word calling this "inferior" or "slavery". Glory in the blessing that you do not *have* to work (for you who don't) and can spend your days in your home with your children.[9]

## Responsibilities of the Couple

First, *the couple is to procreate.*

> *God blessed them; and God said to them, "Be fruitful and multiply, and fill the earth, and subdue it; and rule over the fish of the sea and over the birds of the sky and over every living thing that moves on the earth."*

> Genesis 1:28

Let me preface this by saying that I understand not every couple is physically able to have children. Whether because of age, surgery, or other physical concern, you may have been told that you will never have children. Understand that all sickness and physical concerns are the result of the curse that sin

---

[9] Please note that because of today's fast-paced living and fluctuating economies, many women are required to work outside the home to help provide income for a reasonable standard of living. This is indeed noble and needed at times, and I am not looking down in any way on those wives and mothers who must work. I am simply saying that it is God's intention for wives and mothers to be able to fulfill their responsibilities at home without the pressures of the outside world breaking through and forcing additional work upon them.

brought upon humanity. While it may not be directly related to you or even your family, your inability to conceive, if physically uncontrollable, is a part of the curse of sin on our race. Why you are affected specifically is a question I cannot and will not attempt to answer. I do know that God never does anything without purpose, and that many times His purpose is never revealed to us.

Let me also say that procreation is not the primary reason for marriage. It is not even the primary responsibility of a couple. Marriage is the solemn example of Christ's relationship to the Church. Procreation is simply for the population of this planet. Once life here is done, we will apparently be asexual beings like angels (see Matthew 22:30; Mark 12:25). We have already noted that those couples who are able to have children have the added responsibility of rearing those children "in the discipline and instruction of the Lord" (Ephesians 6:4).

Secondly, *each partner is to fulfill the other's sexual needs.*

> [3]*The husband must fulfill his duty to his wife, and likewise also the wife to her husband.* [4]*The wife does not have authority over her own body, but the husband does; and*

> *likewise also the husband does not have au-*
> *thority over his own body, but the wife does.*
> *⁵Stop depriving one another, except by*
> *agreement for a time, so that you may devote*
> *yourselves to prayer, and come together*
> *again so that Satan will not tempt you be-*
> *cause of your lack of self-control.*

1 Corinthians 7:3-5

Paul stated that once married, each of us is no longer in control of our own body – our partner is! Apparently, the people in Corinth, even the Christians, were very much like people today. It is not hard to find marital advice referring to "withholding" sex from one's spouse in order to gain some sort of power leverage in the marriage. Marriage is not supposed to be a power struggle! God has ordained the "chain of command", if you will, in this covenant relationship. These fights for the upper hand are a result of the curse (Genesis 3:16). Paul had to tell these Christians to stop using sex in this way, "depriving one another" of the gift God has given to married couples.

The only exception is when both partners mutually consent to abstain from sex for a time of spiritual renewal, with the understanding that the abstinence is temporary. After this set time of prayer, they are to come back together "so that Satan will not tempt" them with sexual impurity.

Thirdly, *the couple is to work to stay together.*

> [10]But to the married I give instructions, not I, but the Lord, that the wife should not leave her husband [11](but if she does leave, she must remain unmarried, or else be reconciled to her husband), and that the husband should not divorce his wife.

> 1 Corinthians 7:10-11

This comes just a few verses down the page. Since we are about to begin the study of divorce, I will say only this here: marriage was designed to be for life. While it definitely takes work to do, this is God's intention. Each couple must be prepared to do what it takes to stay together once married. Otherwise, *don't get married!*

# PART TWO

# DIVORCE

# CHAPTER FOUR
## DIVORCE IN THE OLD TESTAMENT

## Its Beginnings

We cannot say for sure when or where the first divorce took place. We have already seen that marriage itself was instituted by God in the Garden of Eden (Genesis 2:18-25). Divorce, however, has no recorded beginning in Scripture. In fact, at the first mention of divorce, it already seems to be common.

> *They [the priests, vs. 1] shall not take a woman who is profaned by harlotry, nor shall they take a **woman divorced from her husband**; for he is holy to his God...A widow, **or a divorced woman**, or one who is profaned by harlotry, these he [the High Priest, vs. 10] may not take; but rather he is to marry a virgin of his own people,*

Leviticus 21:7, 14

In the books of Genesis and Exodus, divorce is never mentioned. But Moses' remaining three books, we find five references to divorce or divorced people[1], all of them giving the sense that divorce was not something new, but rather an ordinary occurrence in Israel.

## Allowed by Moses

I just stated that three of the five books of Moses mention divorce. However, there is only one passage in the Law of Moses where it is specifically addressed. Whether God commanded Moses to approach the topic or whether Moses did it on his own is something we will address in a later chapter. Suffice it to say here that it is in the Bible and was inspired by God's Holy Spirit and is profitable for our study (see 2 Peter 1:19-21; 2 Timothy 3:16-17).

> *[1]When a man takes a wife and marries her, and it happens that she finds no favor in his eyes because he has found some indecency in her, and he writes her a certificate of divorce and puts it in her hand and sends her out from his house, [2]and she leaves his house and goes and becomes another man's wife, [3]and if the latter husband turns against her and writes her a certificate of divorce and puts it in her hand and sends her out of his*

---

[1] Leviticus 21:7, 14; 22:13; Numbers 30:9; Deuteronomy 22:19, 29; 24:1-4

> house, or if the latter husband dies who took
> her to be his wife, ⁴then her former husband
> who sent her away is not allowed to take her
> again to be his wife, since she has been de-
> filed; for that is an abomination before the
> LORD, and you shall not bring sin on the
> land which the LORD your God gives you
> as an inheritance.

Deuteronomy 24:1-4

Let us note, first of all, that divorce is not commanded in this passage. Nowhere does Moses say, "You *must* divorce her." We also do not find unfettered permission for divorce. Moses does not say, "You *may* divorce her." What we see in Deuteronomy 24 is a *regulation* on divorces that were already occurring among the Israelites. The problem he addressed was that the divorces in Israel were unregulated. There seems to have been no stipulation regarding acceptable and unacceptable grounds for their divorces. Though their marriages were controlled, their divorces apparently were not.

Secondly, note that, just because this passage is included in the Holy Scriptures, it does not mean that God changed His mind about the permanence of marriage. Rather it shows His justice and orderliness. In effect He is saying, "Fine; if you are going to keeping divorcing each other, breaking up the marriages that I instituted, I'm going to put some restrictions on it. You have to do it My way." In actuality, we have here a bit of divine permission, since God did not put an absolute end to all divorces. John R. W. Stott stated it this way: "[Divorce was] *a divine concession to human weakness.*"[2]

Herein lies the first principle you may find difficult to reconcile with your current understanding about divorce: *God has never said, "Thou shalt not divorce."* It's not there; it never was. In fact, He also never called it sin. Divorce is *caused by* sin, but it is not, in and of itself, a sin when done according to God's guidelines. Understand that, beginning in the Mosaic Law, God has made allowances for divorce. Please do not get hung up here because there is much more to study about this subject. Just be sure to make a mental note that divorce is nowhere prohibited in the Old Testament Law; in fact, it is allowed as long as a divinely-ordered procedure is followed.

Let's consider what regulations God put into force. I have already said that divorces were occurring with no apparent grounds. Moses addressed that first.

---

[2] quoted in Swindoll, p. 20.

> *When a man takes a wife and marries her,*
> *and it happens that she finds no favor in his*
> *eyes because he has found some indecency in*
> *her, and he writes her a certificate of divorce*
> *and puts it in her hand and sends her out*
> *from his house...*

Deuteronomy 24:1

If a man found something wrong or shameful with his wife after they were married, he would divorce her. Let's ponder the grounds for such a divorce: "she [found] no favor in his eyes because he...found some indecency in her". The Hebrew word translated "favor" also means "grace, elegance". Today we might say that she didn't charm him anymore. Why? "He...found some indecency in her." Again we look at the Hebrew text for an explanation. "Indecency" (or "uncleanness", KJV) is one translation from the Hebrew word which also means "nakedness, indecency". In fact, of the 54 times it is used in the Hebrew Old Testament, the King James translators used the English "nakedness" 51 times. Figuratively, it also means "shameful exposure". So he was no longer charmed by her because something about her had become exposed to him, and possibly even open to public knowledge.[3]

If her husband divorced her (under the regulations Moses outlined here), the woman was permitted to marry someone else (vs. 2). However, if this man did not like something about her either (the same grounds as the first husband), and he divorced her, the restriction was that she could not return to her former husband lest they "bring sin on the land" (vs. 4). According to the sanctimonious (though unbiblical) idea that "all divorce is wrong", this passage sounds like a soap opera! Not only was there a divorce, but a remarriage and another divorce, too!

I should point out here that adultery was not the reason for either divorce. We are not told the reason in detail, only what was pointed out above. However, if the wife were committing adultery (causing the husband to dislike her), she and her male partner would likely have been put to death the first time

---

[3] This gives us an interesting perspective on why Joseph was called a "righteous man" (Matthew 1:19) – instead of making a big scene because of Mary's pregnancy, "planned to send her away [divorce her] secretly."

(Deuteronomy 22:22). We never would have seen the second marriage or divorce.[4]

There are five elements of this legal divorce that should be noted here, before we leave this passage.

First, *there must be a serious cause for the divorce* (vs. 1). On this Matthew Henry expounds:

> It was not sufficient to say that he did not like her, or that he liked another better, but he must show cause for his dislike; something that made her disagreeable and unpleasant to him, though it might not make her so to another... Whatever is meant by it, doubtless it was something considerable; so that their modern doctors [Pharisees] erred who allowed divorce for every cause, though ever so trivial, Mt. 19:3.[5]

Secondly, *the woman was to be given a legal bill of divorcement* (vs. 1). This was doubtless for a number of reasons. It was so that it was formally in writing, rather than just by

---

[4] Even if no one had actually caught them in the act of adultery, there was a test to see if this sin had been committed so that justice could be meted out (Numbers 5:11-31).

[5] Henry, p. 266.

word of mouth. It would have been drawn up by an official of some sort, possibly with witnesses. The official may have judged whether the husband's complaint was serious enough grounds for a legal divorce. It would protect the woman, who could produce the divorce papers if ever accused of adultery against her ex-husband. Additionally, having to go through the whole procedure may cause the husband to decide for himself that he was acting too hastily, decreasing the number of divorces that were actually legalized.

Thirdly, *the husband must extend a formal dismissal* (vs. 1). This may have included some financial provision for her when she left, though that is not defined here.[6]

Fourthly, *the ex-wife and, presumably, the ex-husband were free to remarry* (vs. 2). Since we are not yet to our full discussion on remarriage, I will just point out that under God's regulations, there was no prohibition on remarriage after the divorce was finalized. The ex-wife obviously remarried, and we assume that the ex-husband was free to do likewise.

Fifthly, *former spouses could not be reconciled if remarriage has occurred* (vs. 4). Again I

---

[6] *Ibid.*

turn to Matthew Henry for his practical consideration:

> ...or perhaps it was intended to prevent men's rashness in putting away their wives; for the wife that was divorced would be apt, in revenge, to marry another immediately, and perhaps the husband that divorced her, how much soever he thought to better himself by another choice, would find the next worse, and something in her more disagreeable, so that he would wish for his first wife again. "No" (says this law) "you shall not have her, you should have kept her when you had her."[7]

## Honorable to God

"OK," you may be thinking, "I can see where God has allowed divorce, but isn't it stretching it a little bit to say that He can actually *honor* it?" To which I must answer: if we stay only in Deuteronomy 24, yes it is. Though divorce is allowed and regulated by Moses, it is not considered honorable by the Mosaic Law. We must continue our journey through the Old Testament to see this principle.

---

[7] *Ibid.*, pp. 266-7.

Let us jump ahead in time about 1,000 years to 458 B.C. It was "the seventh year of Artaxerxes Longimanus"[8] (Ezra 7:8), and Jewish exiles had just returned from Persia to Israel for the second time. Allow me to insert a quote here which will bring to light the importance of this history to our subject at hand.

> The narrative [in Ezra's book] resumes in the first person, relating the report of the Jewish officials that many of the people, including priests and Levites, had intermarried with people of the land (9:1f.) After Ezra's fast (vv. 3-5) and long prayer (vv. 6-15), a large assembly gathered round him and in great remorse offered to divorce their foreign wives, summoning Ezra to supervise the task according to the law (10:1-5).[9]

Now the connection with our topic becomes obvious. The people had been

---

[8] Leon J. Wood, *The Prophets of Israel* (Grand Rapids: Baker, 1979), p. 374.

[9] William Sanford La Sor, David Allan Hubbard, Frederic William Bush. *Old Testament Survey: The Message, Form, and Background of the Old Testament* (Grand Rapids: Eerdmans, 1982), p. 641. (Hereafter cited as OTS.)

brought face to face with conviction of their sin – they had married Gentile wives.

Just before the people of Israel first went into their promised land, they were given strict instructions regarding their dealings with the people already in the land.

> *"When the LORD your God brings you into the land where you are entering to possess it, and clears away many nations before you, the Hittites and the Girgashites and the Amorites and the Canaanites and the Perizzites and the Hivites and the Jebusites, seven nations greater and stronger than you, 2and when the LORD your God delivers them before you and you defeat them, then you shall utterly destroy them. You shall make no covenant with them and show no favor to them. 3Furthermore, you shall not intermarry with them; you shall not give your daughters to their sons, nor shall you take their daughters for your sons. 4For they will turn your sons away from following Me to serve other gods; then the anger of the LORD will be kindled against you and He will quickly destroy you."*

Deuteronomy 7:1-4

Notice that the Israelites were to "make no covenant with" the people of the land. (Remember that marriage is a *covenant* between two people.) And just in case they didn't pick up on all of the subtle ramifications of that command, Moses unmistakably states that they were to "not intermarry with them." How much more plain could he have been? Yet they didn't listen, and 1,000 years later, they were still intermarrying with foreigners, contaminating the Jewish bloodlines.

It was obvious that they had broken God's law, and now they were repentant, wanting to right their wrongs. Their only solution was to divorce those wives (10:2-3). The rest of the chapter details the proceedings of this very action, including the account that those who did not divorce their wives were excommunicated from the congregation of Israel.

According to the unbiblical idea that all divorce is wrong, we would expect fire from Heaven to fall on these 113 new divorcés for this heinous act of disregard for God's holy institution. But there is none. In fact, we see nothing but God's blessing as they unify and begin to rebuild Jerusalem.[10] These Israelites were never condemned for their divorces. In fact, God was able to use them because they had reconciled themselves to Him through

---

[10] The Hebrew Scriptures have Ezra and Nehemiah as one book. After this mass divorce is finalized (Ezra 10), the very next chapter is Nehemiah 1, when God begins to work to have His city rebuilt.

divorce. This is a beautiful example that divorce, though caused by sin, is not sinful of itself.

## Does God have a "Past"?

At this point, some of you may be thinking, "What does he mean by 'past'?" Others are already in defensive mode: "I don't like where he's heading with this." The following discussion may just shake the entire foundation of how you view this topic, especially if you have never studied it like this before. Let me assure you that this is OK. This is what Bible study is all about: to have our eyes and hearts opened to God's Word for what it says, putting aside all previous opinions that are based on tradition rather than solid Bible teaching. Let us return to Jay Adams for an introduction to these often overlooked passages.

> In a number of passages, God speaks of His relationship to His OT covenant people as a marriage. As the NT makes clear (Eph. 5:22-23), this is more than a mere analogy; rather, the biblical norm for Christian marriage is found in the relationship of Christ to His church (the prototype of which was the relationship of God to His bride, Israel): as Chr-

ist...so   too   the   husband;   as   the
church...so too the wife.[11]

As I print them here, I ask that you
carefully mull over these passages in your own
mind and heart.   Use your own copy of the
Scriptures and read their contexts.

## God covenanted in marriage

> *"Then I passed by you and saw you, and be-*
> *hold, you were at the time for love; so I*
> *spread My skirt over you and covered your*
> *nakedness. I also swore to you and entered*
> *into a covenant with you so that you became*
> *Mine," declares the Lord GOD.*

Ezekiel 16:8

> *"Go and proclaim in the ears of Jerusalem,*
> *saying, 'Thus says the LORD, "I remember*
> *concerning you the devotion of your youth,*
> *the love of your betrothals, your following*
> *after Me in the wilderness, through a land*
> *not sown."'"*

Jeremiah 2:2

God entered into a (marriage) covenant
with Israel at Mount Sinai (see Exodus 34:10-
28).   Notice that this was not an unconditional

---

[11] Adams, p. 71.

covenant. In order to uphold her end of the bargain, Israel had to "observe" (vs. 11) the commands given to her at the mountain. If she did not obey them, she would breach the contract. According to Jeremiah 2:2, the Israelites were faithful during their years of wandering in the wilderness.

## Israel broke her covenant vows

> *"For on every high hill and under every green tree you have lain down as a harlot."*

Jeremiah 2:20b

> *6Then the LORD said to me in the days of Josiah the king, "Have you seen what faithless Israel did? She went up on every high hill and under every green tree, and she was a harlot there. 7I thought, 'After she has done all these things she will return to Me'; but she did not return, and her treacherous sister Judah saw it...9Because of the lightness of her harlotry, she polluted the land and committed adultery with stones and trees."*

Jeremiah 3:6-7, 9

> *"For she said, 'I will go after my lovers, who give me my bread and my water, my wool and my flax, my oil and my drink.'...When she used to offer sacrifices to them and adorn herself with her earrings and jewelry, and*

> *follow her lovers, so that she forgot Me,"*
> *declares the LORD.*

Hosea 2:5b, 13b

> [17]*"The Babylonians came to her to the bed of*
> *love and defiled her with their harlotry. And*
> *when she had been defiled by them, she be-*
> *came disgusted with them.* [18]*She uncovered*
> *her harlotries and uncovered her nakedness;*
> *then I became disgusted with her, as I had*
> *become disgusted with her sister.* [19]*Yet she*
> *multiplied her harlotries, remembering the*
> *days of her youth, when she played the har-*
> *lot in the land of Egypt."*

Ezekiel 23:17-19

Israel broke her covenant with God by going after other gods ("lovers"). After entering the land of Canaan, she refused to follow God's command to eliminate the other peoples. The book of Judges gives us one tragic story after another of Israel's continual following after other gods. The prophets are full of warnings and admonitions to return to the true God, but she has never done so fully.

### God filed for divorce

> *"And I saw that for all the adulteries of*
> *faithless Israel, I had sent her away and giv-*
> *en her a writ of divorce..."*

Jeremiah 3:8a

> "Contend with your mother, contend, for
> she is not my wife, and I am not her hus-
> band; and let her put away her harlotry from
> her face and her adultery from between her
> breasts,"

Hosea 2:2

This is where many of us will involunta-
rily recoil. Can we really say that God has
been divorced? If we take Scripture literally,
then the answer has to be "Yes". Though He
many times offered to receive Israel back, and
though she did return many times, those
periods of her history were brief, slight transi-
tions where she got back on her feet only to
follow false gods yet again.

Finally God said, "Enough. You have
proven over time that you do not truly love
Me; there is someone else in My place. Here
are your official divorce papers; follow whom
you will." As the offended Husband, God had
the right to divorce His unfaithful bride, and
He finally exercised that right. He was freed of
His covenant with them because of their sin.

Let me re-emphasize something I said
earlier: divorce is *not* a sin (when done properly); it is *caused by* sin. God cannot sin and did
not sin by divorcing Israel. Her sin allowed
Him to do so. On Jeremiah 3:8a, commentators
Keil and Delitzsch translate

> literally: that for all the reasons, because the backslider had committed adultery, *I put her away and gave her a bill of divorce;* yet the faithless Judah feared not.[12] [italics added]

## *Israel's future reconciliation*

Fortunately for Israel, that is not the end of the story. Let us look at just a couple more passages.

> [1]*"Return, O Israel, to the LORD your God, for you have stumbled because of your iniquity. [2]Take words with you and return to the LORD. Say to Him, 'Take away all iniquity and receive us graciously, that we may present the fruit of our lips.'"*

Hosea 14:1-2

> [6]*"For the LORD has called you, like a wife forsaken and grieved in spirit, even like a wife of one's youth when she is rejected,"* says your God. [7]*"For a brief moment I forsook you, but with great compassion **I will gather you.** [8]In an outburst of anger I hid My face from you for a moment, but with everlasting lovingkindness **I will have compassion on you,"** says the LORD your Redeemer.*

Isaiah 54:6-8

---

[12] K&D, vol. 8, p. 86.

In His ever-gracious way, God still calls to Israel to be reconciled to Him. Even in all of her unfaithfulness Israel never actually "married" another god, permanently leaving the true God. Because of this, He patiently awaits her return. Through His prophets He has given us a glimpse of the future: Israel will finally return in repentance, never to leave again. At that time God will once again turn His attention to her, welcoming her back with open arms, accepting her as His pure, undefiled "wife of [their] youth".

## God's Personal Opinion

As we close this chapter we dare not overlook one last passage, one where God bares His heart and gives His true feelings about divorce.

When approached with the question of divorce, many Christians will quote one phrase out of this otherwise little-known Old Testament passage. Let's see what they find so interesting here.

> [13]*"This is another thing you do: you cover the altar of the LORD with tears, with weeping and with groaning, because He no longer regards the offering or accepts it with favor from your hand.* [14]*"Yet you say, 'For*

> *what reason?' Because the LORD has been a witness between you and the wife of your youth, against whom you have dealt treacherously, though she is your companion and your wife by covenant. [15]"But not one has done so who has a remnant of the Spirit. And what did that one do while he was seeking a godly offspring? Take heed then to your spirit, and let no one deal treacherously against the wife of your youth. [16]"For I hate divorce," says the LORD, the God of Israel, "and him who covers his garment with wrong," says the LORD of hosts. "So take heed to your spirit, that you do not deal treacherously."*

> Malachi 2:13-16

*Aha!* God *does* hate divorce. But He Himself is divorced. How can this be?

One of the first rules of Bible interpretation is that we must use the context of a passage to determine its interpretation. We do this by comparing the verse (or verses) in question to the immediate surrounding verses, chapters, the whole book, and the Bible as a whole. Because one part of Scripture will never contradict another, we are able to compare different passages on a subject and find explanations that the immediate passage may not fully give. Such is the case in Malachi chapter 2.

If you read through the entire recorded prophecy of Malachi (go ahead and do it now; it's short), you will find that he touches on many different topics of which divorce is only one. Additionally, divorce is addressed in only these four verses, and the word "divorce" is mentioned only once in the entire book. While we should not take lightly or disregard what God has to say through Malachi, neither should we base our entire doctrine of divorce on four verses. We must diligently compare this passage to others in order to get its intended context. So what does it say?

God had not been accepting Israel's offerings on the temple altar because of their numerous sins against God, including ingratitude (1:2-5), disrespect / dishonor (1:6-14), ungodly priests (2:1-9), breaking His covenant (2:10-12), improper divorces (2:13-16), robbing God (3:8-9), and arrogance (3:13-15). Not only were their divorces not the only problem, they were not what we would consider the worst problem in the list, and God seems to mention them only in passing ("This is another thing you do", 2:13), not stopping to dwell on them very long.

We have already seen in Deuteronomy 24 that, though divorce was not God's original plan for marriage, He allowed it as long as the people followed His regulations. Even though Malachi prophesied 1,000 years after the Law was established, the people still lived under that Law. So divorce was still permitted with restrictions.

I think verse 14 gives us the reason that it comes up in this prophecy:

> *"Yet you say, 'For what reason?' Because the LORD has been a witness between you and* **the wife of your youth, against whom you have dealt treacherously,** *though she is your companion and your wife by covenant."*

Malachi 2:14

The main problem here was not that they were divorcing their wives, but that they were dealing "treacherously" with them. The Hebrew verb, *bâgad*, is found in the Old Testament:

> forty-seven times, twenty-one times using the participle as a verbal noun to describe the one who deals treacherously. *He is one who does not honor an agreement.* The root in South Arabic means "to deceive." The verb is used to denote unfaithfulness in several different relationships. It is used in connection with

74

[among other things] unfaithfulness in
marriage.[13] [italics, brackets added]

Remember that a marriage is a contract
or covenant, an agreement, solemnized by
vows. The Israelites were making these
agreements before God, then dealing "treacherously" with, or not keeping their vows to,
their wives. The problem God was addressing
here was not so much their divorces, but rather
their breaking of vows which led to divorce.

OK, but how do we get around verse
sixteen? It still has God on record as saying
that He hates divorce. I'm sure He does hate
divorce. It was never a part of His original
plan for marriage. Divorce was the result of
mankind corrupting God's perfect establishment, so He has good reason to hate it. But
again, He does not condemn it. As in Deuteronomy 24, God does not ban divorce in this
passage; He simply expresses His displeasure
toward the actions leading up to the divorces:
the breaking of vows.

This brings up one more point from this
passage: God hates *the cause of divorce*. He
hates the *effect* that divorce has on people. He
hates that His perfect institution of marriage is

---

[13] *TWOT*, "198", pp. 89-90.

spoiled *by* divorce. But, He *does not hate* the divorce proceedings. He *does not hate* the legal divorce papers. And He definitely *does not hate* those people who have been divorced. We must be careful to observe this distinction as does God. Too often we confuse the divorce and the divorcees, and abandon the persons involved when God never does. If we are going to follow God's pattern in this matter, we must intentionally separate the divorce and its cause from the people affected by it. Yes, God hates the fact that they sinned. He hates the fact that their marriage is dissolved. But He never hates them, and He is always "faithful...to forgive" (1 John 1:9) all sin confessed in humility to Him.

# Chapter Five
# Divorce in the New Testament

As we move into the New Testament, let us quickly refresh our minds with what we found in the Old Testament regarding divorce:

1. Divorce is man's establishment. God instituted permanence in marriage.
2. God neither bans nor condemns divorce. In fact, He allows it as long as it is done properly, according to His established guidelines.
3. A proper divorce can be more honorable to God than an improper marriage.
4. God, Himself, has divorced Israel because of her unfaithfulness to Him.
5. Though God hates divorce, including its cause (sin, broken vows) and its effects (marriages dissolved,

people hurt), He never hates the people involved.


In the New Testament we find four primary passages dealing with our subject. The first two record the words of Jesus and are both found in Matthew (5:31-32; 19:3-9).[1] The other two are from Paul (Romans 7:1-3; 1 Corinthians 7:1-40). Let me give a brief summary of each of these passages, and then we will study them further in the following chapters and see what principles are available for us.


## Matthew 5:31-32

This was essentially a passing comment by Jesus on divorce. We find this passage in the Sermon on the Mount, where Jesus was introducing His listeners (and readers) to the kingdom of God. If He would have entitled this sermon, it may have been something like "The Ways Things are Supposed to (and

---

[1] Mark 10:2-12 is a parallel passage to Matthew 19:3-9 and does not give all of the information that Matthew does. We will use Matthew's account as a primary passage.

Someday Will) Be". In it we find how different His Kingdom will be in comparison to the world in which we currently live. Because He was going to be referring to the Old Testament writings, Jesus prefaced His teaching by saying,

> *Do not think that I came to abolish the Law or the Prophets; I did not come to abolish but to fulfill.*

Matthew 5:17

He was about to say some things that the Jews were not expecting, and He wanted to be sure that they understood that these were not new teachings against the Law, but rather the ultimate intention of that Law.

In the verses immediately surrounding our two verses on divorce, look at how Jesus addresses these various topics:

- Murder – "You have heard…But I say to you…" (vs. 21-22)
- Adultery – "You have heard…but I say to you…" (vs. 27-28)
- Divorce – "It was said…but I say to you…" (vs. 31-32)
- Vows – "You have heard…but I say to you…" (vs. 33-34)
- Personal revenge – "You have heard…But I say to you…" (vs. 38-39)

- Personal relations – "You have heard…But I say to you…" (vs. 43-44)

He knew that their traditions and the things they had been taught had been perverted over time. Rabbis and other commentators had interpreted God's Word the way they desired, and their teaching, even if the words were quoted correctly, had lost its true meaning and intention. In order to "fulfill" the Law and Prophets, Jesus had to first teach what the Law and Prophets meant in their teachings.

In this passage, Jesus was not attempting to give a complete teaching on divorce, covering all aspects.[2] He was simply correcting what they already understood from their tradition and false teaching.

### Matthew 19:3-9

This passage contains what is considered to be Jesus' primary teaching on divorce.

---

[2] Because this was never meant to be the full doctrine of divorce (just like the Old Testament passages in the last chapter), we must be careful to not let this passage stand on its own. What we learn here *must* be understood in light of the other passages on divorce and balanced with them.

The subject was brought up by the Pharisees who were trying to trap Jesus in His own words. Even in a quick reading of the passage, it is obvious that Jesus actually spent more time discussing marriage than divorce. Again, this is not an all-inclusive teaching on this subject. Jesus took only what time was necessary to answer the specific question about Deuteronomy 24:1. As with Matthew 5:31-32, we should not take all of our doctrine from these few verses.

## Romans 7:1-3

While all of the New Testament books indeed teach the Christian doctrines, Romans is by far the greatest theological work of the New Testament, giving depth that the other books do not. With a glance at the outline of the book, we would not expect to find a dissertation on divorce in the middle of the deep theology that Romans contains. And, in fact, we don't. In these three verses, divorce is not really the topic of discussion; Paul was actually writing about the relationship of Christians to the Old Testament Law. He simply used marriage and divorce as an illustration. However, a principle is given that we must consider in our study.

We have already read this passage in chapter two, referring to the permanence of marriage. We will take another look later, focusing on the divorce issue.

### 1 Corinthians 7:1-40

This is Paul's primary teaching on our subject. This is because he touched on all three aspects of our study – marriage, divorce and remarriage. In doing so, he referred back to Jesus' words in Matthew, clarifying and applying His teachings. So this will also be our primary text as we get into the New Testament teaching on divorce.

# CHAPTER SIX
# DIVORCE IN CHRISTIAN MARRIAGES
# (PART ONE)

> *10But to the married I give instructions, not I, but the Lord, that the wife should not leave her husband 11(but if she does leave, she must remain unmarried, or else be reconciled to her husband), and that the husband should not divorce his wife.*

> 1 Corinthians 7:10-11

You may wonder, even if Paul's writing is good, since Jesus talked on the subject, why we would look at 1 Corinthians first as we set out to see the New Testament detail on divorce. Jay Adams explains the reason:

> because so many of the key words and concepts are found there, and because in it there is a comparison and contrast between the two possible divorce situations that the NT considers, and because Paul interprets the words of Jesus and places them in their proper context, I

Corinthians 7 is an excellent starting point.[1]

## Two Scenarios

Dr. Adams referred to the first aspect that we must understand about the New Testament teaching on divorce: *the New Testament deals with only two possible scenarios for divorce.* Paul shares these two scenarios in verses 10 and 12:

> [10]*But to the married I give instructions, not I, but the Lord, that…*[12]*But to the rest I say, not the Lord, that…*

1 Corinthians 7:10, 12

Many people have a problem with these two verses because it sounds like Paul is giving some information from God (inspired – "not I, but the Lord") and some information from his own opinion (non-inspired – "I say, not the Lord"). If we take 2 Timothy 3:16 to be true that "all Scripture is inspired by God", then we eliminate this from being a problem. However, it does bring up a valid question that should be answered before we take any doctrine from this passage: what does Paul mean by these two phrases? There seems to be only one

---

[1] Adams, p. 36.

explanation that supports both the inerrancy of God's Word and the literal words that Paul dictated. In short[2], for the first scenario, Paul is simply teaching the same doctrine that Jesus taught previously ("not I, but the Lord"; see Matthew 5:31-32; 19:3-9). Paul was not going to add to or subtract from what Jesus had already taught. The second scenario, however, had never before been addressed. So Paul could say, "I say, not the Lord [i.e., Jesus never gave a teaching on this, so this is not a quote like the first one was]".

It turns out that Paul's scenarios are not situations, but couples. There are only two types of couples that fall within the scope of the New Testament teaching on divorce: 1) two Christians are married to each other – Jesus spoke to this issue Himself[3]; and 2) a Christian

---

[2] If you would like support from other Bible scholars for this view, see the first section of "Appendix: First Corinthians 7 Examined".

[3] In Matthew 5:31-32, Jesus was introducing the kingdom of God to God's people – the Jews (see this discussion in the previous chapter). Since Israel as a nation rejected Jesus as Messiah (Matthew 12:1-21), Israel has been set aside for the current time. During our current dispensation, Christians – consisting of both Jews and Gentiles – are God's people. Thus Paul could use Jesus'

is married to a non-Christian – Paul was the first Bible writer to address this.

## Couple #1 – Two Christians

> *10But to the married I give instructions, not I, but the Lord, that the wife should not leave her husband 11(but if she does leave, she must remain unmarried, or else be reconciled to her husband), and that the husband should not divorce his wife.*

1 Corinthians 7:10-11

> *31"It was said, 'WHOEVER SENDS HIS WIFE AWAY, LET HIM GIVE HER A CERTIFICATE OF DIVORCE'; 32but I say to you that everyone who divorces his wife, except for the reason of unchastity, makes her commit adultery; and whoever marries a divorced woman commits adultery.*

Matthew 5:31-32

In case you didn't recognize it, Jesus was quoting part of Deuteronomy 24:1. You may not remember it exactly like that. Remember that, though the Old Testament words had been copied on paper carefully, they were not always taught as they were originally

words to the Jews in direct reference to the Gentile Christians in Corinth.

given, because the rabbis and commentators added their own meanings when they taught. So Jesus was quoting what His listeners had been taught, rather than the Scriptures directly, thus the "misquote". So let's look at the particulars of His statement.[4] There are really two questions that must be answered to give us the information we seek. The first is *what had Jesus' listeners been taught about divorce?* The second, *what was Jesus teaching?*

I said in the last chapter that God's original teachings had been perverted over time by the rabbis and other teachers of the Old Testament Scriptures, but I never mentioned what those perversions were. A comparison of Matthew 19:3-9 and Deuteronomy 24:1-4 gives us those discrepancies. I have bolded the phrases that do not line up with each other in these passages; italics are all original.

---

[4] We will dissect Jesus' "exception clause" in chapter eight, so I'll not touch on it here.

| *Jewish tradition* | *Original teaching* |
|---|---|
| 1. A man could divorce his wife for <u>any</u> reason. | 1. There had to be <u>reasonable grounds</u> for divorce. |

> *Is it lawful for a man to divorce his wife for **any reason at all**?*
>
> Matthew 19:3

> *When a man takes a wife and marries her, and it happens that she finds no favor in his eyes **because he has found some indecency in her**...*
>
> Deuteronomy 24:1a

| 2. Moses <u>commanded</u> the husbands to divorce their wives. | 2. Moses only <u>regulated</u> the divorces that were occurring. |
|---|---|

> ***Why then did Moses command** to give her a certificate of divorce and send her away?*
>
> Matthew 19:7

> *When a man takes a wife... and it happens... and he writes... and sends her... and she leaves... **then [he] is not allowed**...*
>
> Deuteronomy 24:1-2, 4

In answer to our first question (what had they been taught by handed-down tradition?), apparently there were no required grounds for a legal divorce, and Moses had, in fact, commanded them to divorce their wives for even the slightest thing. Now even the most unlearned person could not get those teachings out of what Moses actually said, unless they were purposely trying to make God's Word say what they wanted it to. It sounds very much like many of our so-called "Bible preachers" today, doesn't it? Tell the people what they want to hear so they can feel good about themselves and not have guilt over their deliberate sins. Paul says this about these people: "wanting to have their ears tickled, they will accumulate for themselves teachers in accordance to their own desires" (2 Timothy 4:3).

The answer to our second question will give us Jesus' take on these erroneous, traditional teachings. The Pharisees actually put it forth in two questions, which Jesus answered directly. Here is how the conversation went:

> [3]*Some Pharisees came to Jesus, testing Him and asking, "Is it lawful for a man to divorce his wife for any reason at all?"* [4]*And He answered and said, "Have you not read that He who created them from the beginning MADE THEM MALE AND FEMALE,* [5]*and said, 'FOR THIS REASON A MAN SHALL LEAVE HIS FATHER AND MOTHER AND BE JOINED TO HIS WIFE, AND THE TWO SHALL BECOME ONE FLESH'?* [6]*"So they are no longer two, but one flesh. What therefore God*

> has joined together, let no man separate."
> *7They said to Him, "Why then did Moses command to* GIVE HER A CERTIFICATE OF DIVORCE AND SEND *her* AWAY?" *8He said to them, "Because of your hardness of heart Moses permitted you to divorce your wives; but from the beginning it has not been this way. 9"And I say to you, whoever divorces his wife, except for immorality, and marries another woman commits adultery."*

Matthew 19:3-9

The first false teaching was that divorce was acceptable without reasonable ground ("for any reason at all", vs. 3). Jesus corrected this by going back to the establishment of marriage. He reminded them (using the Scriptures in which they considered themselves to be experts) that when God established marriage, His pattern was 1) *"male and female"* (only two partners, vs. 4; see Genesis 1:27); 2) *"the two shall become one flesh"* (two individuals becoming one person, vs. 5; see Genesis 2:24); and 3) *"God has joined together"* (God brought her to him, vs. 6; see Genesis 2:22). Nowhere in His direct answer to this question did Jesus debate acceptable grounds for divorce.[5] He

---

[5] Even His "exception clause" is not mentioned until a few verses later. Divorce, under any circumstances, was never part of God's plan for His people.

simply said that divorce is not God's way. God's pattern for marriage is not one of those "rules that are made to be broken". He didn't set it up that way.

The second question they posed showed the second false teaching of the day: Moses commanded them to divorce. Again, Jesus pulled no punches in His answer. (Don't you love how He gets right to the point?)

> He said to them, "Because of your hardness of heart Moses permitted you to divorce your wives; but from the beginning it has not been this way.

Matthew 19:8

"Don't even try to blame this on Moses! It was your own fault! Moses didn't *command* divorce; he *permitted* it. And only because you were so stubborn that you were doing it anyway. He was just trying to keep you legal!" Jesus did not condemn Moses for allowing divorce, but He was also sure to insert that "from the beginning it has not been this way."

> The purpose of this law was to prevent hasty divorce, discourage adultery, and preserve marriage. The people of Jesus' day took this *permission to* divorce as a *promotion of* divorce, but Jesus reminded them that such was not God's original plan (Matthew 19:4-6), and that divorce

> was allowed by Moses only because of
> the 'hardness of your hearts' (Matthew
> 19:8).[6] [italics added]

To summarize Jesus' teaching on this first couple (two Christians), God never intended for His people to divorce for any reason at all. No matter the tradition or misunderstanding of His Word, that was not His established pattern. Paul adds just a little bit to this in the parentheses of 1 Corinthians 7:11: *"but if she does leave, she must remain unmarried, or else be reconciled to her husband"*. We will discuss this in much more detail later, but for now make a mental note that the two people under consideration are both professing Christians, in fellowship with God, living their lives according to His will for them.

> The integrity and permanence of the in-
> dividual home is of such great impor-
> tance that God made it plain from the
> beginning that marriage was intended
> to be permanent until death. It is true,
> of course, that with marriage as well as
> with all other human activities, "God
> hath made man upright; but they have

---

[6] Jerry Falwell, ed. *The Liberty Annotated Study Bible* (Lynchburg, VA: Old Time Gospel Hour, 1988), p. 336.

sought out many inventions" (Ecclesiastes 7:29). Polygamy, concubinage, polyandry, easy divorce, adultery, promiscuity, and other distortions of the marriage covenant have permeated many cultures; but, as the Lord Jesus said: "From the beginning it was not so" (Matthew 19:8).[7]

---

[7] Morris, p. 102.

# CHAPTER SEVEN
## DIVORCE IN MIXED MARRIAGES

As we saw in the last chapter, though Paul could quote Jesus' teachings about divorce between Christians, no one had yet addressed marriages between a believer and an unbeliever[1], not to mention divorce in those circumstances. In 1 Corinthians 7, Paul covers many aspects about marriage, divorce, and remarriage. Regarding mixed marriages, he says,

> [12]*But to the rest I say, not the Lord, that if any brother has a wife who is an unbeliever, and she consents to live with him, he must not divorce her.* [13]*And a woman who has an unbelieving husband, and he consents to live with her, she must not send her husband away.* [14]*For the unbelieving husband is sanctified through his wife, and the unbe-*

---

[1] An unbeliever is someone who does not believe in Jesus' deity and has not accepted Jesus death as the only sufficient payment to God for his or her personal sin.

> *lieving wife is sanctified through her believ-*
> *ing husband; for otherwise your children are*
> *unclean, but now they are holy.* [15]*Yet if the*
> *unbelieving one leaves, let him leave; the*
> *brother or the sister is not under bondage in*
> *such cases, but God has called us to peace.*
> [16]*For how do you know, O wife, whether you*
> *will save your husband? Or how do you*
> *know, O husband, whether you will save*
> *your wife?*

1 Corinthians 7:12-16

## Couple #2 – One believer, one unbeliever

Because of the covenant before God that is involved in marriage, the Bible nowhere condones the marriage of a believer to an unbeliever. In fact, He specifically condemns it (see 2 Corinthians 6:14ff). In this case, Paul cites a case where either the husband or the wife is a Christian and the other is not.

Again we must emphasize God's original pattern: marriage is to be permanent. No matter the immediate spiritual state of the partners involved, God designed marriage partners to be together for life. Here, Paul commands even mixed marriages to hold to the pattern.

In his first example, the unbelieving spouse, though wanting nothing to do with Christianity (at this time), is also not interested in divorce. He/she wants nothing but to remain married to his/her believing spouse. Paul says, "Great! Stay together." Even in this event God does not command or recommend divorce. In fact, He commands just the opposite: "he **must not** divorce her...she **must not** send her husband away (vs. 12-13, emphasis added).

> The Christian calling did not dissolve the marriage covenant, but bind it the faster, by bringing it back to the original institution, limiting it to two persons, and binding them together for life. The believer is not by faith in Christ loosed from matrimonial bonds to an unbeliever, but is at once bound and made apt to be a better relative.[2]

Wouldn't the Christian be more likely to be built up in a Christian relationship? We would hope so. Wouldn't he/she have a more spiritually-fulfilling relationship with his/her new spouse if he/she were to marry a believer? Yes, probably so. However, God's hands

---

[2] Henry, p. 2256.

are not tied by our mistakes. His perfect will may be delayed by human rebellion, but He always works things out for His own glory. Paul gives us three reasons that it is good for the partners to stay together.

First, *the unbelieving partner "is sanctified by" the believer (vs. 14)*. Because of our typical understanding of sanctification, the question inevitably arises: what does Paul mean that the unbeliever "is sanctified by" the believer? We are taught that to be "sanctified" means "to be set apart; to be made holy". Since initial sanctification happens at salvation, it is used synonymously with salvation at times. Obviously, the husband is not automatically saved when his wife becomes a believer, or vice versa, so what does Paul mean? In his notes on this passage, Albert Barnes answers a question that may have gone through the minds of those new believers in Corinth:

> "Shall I not be POLLUTED by such a connection? Shall I not be defiled, in the eye of God, by living in a close union with a pagan, a sinner, an enemy of God, and an opposer of the gospel?" This objection was natural, and is, doubtless, often felt. To this the apostle replies, "No; the contrary may be true. The connection produces a species of sanctification, or diffuses a kind of holiness over the un-

> believing party by the believing party,
> so far as to render their children holy,
> and therefore it is improper to seek for a
> separation."[3]

Though the unbelieving spouse is not saved based on the other's salvation, the relationship is now made holy because of the Christian.

Secondly, *the children of a mixed marriage are "holy" (vs. 14)*. Again, we understand that God is the sole source of holiness, and that it is applied through a person's individual acceptance of Jesus' salvation. Paul is not contradicting his own teaching of salvation by grace through faith alone (Ephesians 2:8-9). We turn again to Barnes, who continues his discussion on the passage:

> [The children are] Holy in the same sense as the unbelieving husband is SANCTIFIED by the believing wife; for different forms of the same word are usual. That is, they are legitimate. They are not to be branded and treated as bastards, as they would be by your separation. YOU regard them as having been born in lawful wedlock, and they ARE so; and they should be treated as such by their parents, and not be exposed to shame and disgrace by your separation.[4]

---

[3] Barnes, "1 Corinthians 7:14".

[4] *Ibid.*

Thirdly, *the believer is able to be a constant witness to the unbeliever (vs. 16).* Probably the best reason to preserve the marriage when possible is that the believer may be able to show the other Christ. This, however, should never be used as an excuse for a believer to marry an unbeliever at the outset (see 2 Corinthians 6:14ff).

> Paul replied that they were to remain with their unconverted mates so long as their mates were willing to live with them. Salvation does not alter the marriage state; if anything, it ought to enhance the marriage relationship. (Note Peter's counsel to wives with unsaved husbands in 1 Peter 3:1-6.)[5]

## Trouble on the Home Front

> *Yet if the unbelieving one leaves, let him leave; the brother or the sister is not under bondage in such cases, but God has called us to peace.*

1 Corinthians 7:15

In a mixed marriage (one believer and one unbeliever), we have seen that the general

---

[5] Warren W. Wiersbe, *The Bible Exposition Commentary* (Wheaton, IL: Victor Books, 1989), Vol. 1, p. 591.

rule is the same as if both partners were Christians: do what can be done to preserve the marriage. This does come with an exception, however. Here the situation is when one partner becomes a Christian and the unbelieving spouse cannot handle it. For whatever reason, having a Christian marriage partner has completely disrupted the marriage. Perhaps the Christian is being newly convicted for things that the couple used to do together; we are not given any specifics. Suffice it to say that the unbelieving husband or wife is no longer happy and wants to call it quits.

It's sad, but this is an all-too-common occurrence. Many times it is the wife who accepts Jesus Christ as Savior, and the husband wants nothing to do with "religion". He never wanted a "goody-goody" wife who disapproves of his chosen lifestyle, even if she is not blatant about it.

We should take a moment and revisit the passage to which Warren Wiersbe referred earlier.

> *[1]In the same way, you wives, be submissive to your own husbands so that even if any of them are disobedient to the word, they may be won without a word by the behavior of their wives, [2]as they observe your chaste and respectful behavior.*

1 Peter 3:1-2

Apparently, even in Bible times wives were convicted and saved sooner than their husbands. Notice how Peter told these Christian women, and those in the same situation today, to handle their new-found, and possibly difficult, situation: "without a word." Peter did not tell them to preach the gospel around the house. In fact, he commanded just the opposite: let your character do the talking to your husband. There should be a big enough change in the woman's attitude and behavior toward her husband that he cannot help but notice. Primarily, only when he approaches the subject should she share Jesus Christ with him. Interestingly enough, just thirteen verses later Peter admonished each person that "if someone asks about your Christian hope, always be ready to explain it" (1 Peter 3:15b, NLT).

So what is Paul's solution? If the unbelieving spouse wants to leave the marriage, the believer should still try to preserve it. Now there are times that one partner is content to stay in the current marriage, while at the same time "fooling around" on his or her spouse (or worse). Though this partner never states, "I want to leave you", the continual breaking of the covenantal vows indicate that he or she is not interested in reconciling to the original plan for marriage with that partner. If the "leaving" of the unbelieving spouse necessitates a physical move, this ties up the believing partner in a "marriage" in which reconciliation seems nearly impossible. So I have to believe that the unbelieving spouse's "leaving" can be carried out by not only a physical moving out of the house or filing for divorce, but also a lifestyle of "leaving" or breaking the marriage covenant. This may include continued sexual unfaithfulness[6], continued abuse, and possibly many other situations.

If there is no hope of the marriage being preserved (that is, put back into its covenantal form – accomplished through repentance and forgiveness), the believer *must* let the other go ("let him leave") because he or she is not "under bondage in such cases". The word "bondage" here carries the same meaning as the one Paul used in Romans 7:2 – *"For the married woman is bound by law to her husband..."* Just as death frees the living partner from all

---

[6] Remember that sexual unfaithfulness does not *mandate* a divorce; it simply allows for it. Reconciliation is the preferred result.

obligations related to that marriage, when the unbelieving spouse leaves the marriage, the Christian is free to divorce that person, freeing him or her from all marital obligations to the former spouse.

# CHAPTER EIGHT
# DIVORCE IN CHRISTIAN MARRIAGES
# (PART TWO)

Before we pick up where we left off in chapter six, let's recap briefly what we have already learned about divorce in marriages where both partners are Christians:

1. Paul gave us no new teaching beyond what Jesus had already taught.
2. There had to be reasonable grounds for divorce (Deuteronomy 24:1a).
3. However, divorce does not follow God's original pattern for marriage (Genesis 1:27; 2:18-24).

## Jesus' Exception Clause

Anyone who has studied this subject even a little knows that in both of Jesus' statements in Matthew regarding divorce there is a phrase which gives an exception to the general "no divorce" standard. What is that exception?

> *"...but I say to you that everyone who divorces his wife, **except for the reason of unchastity**, makes her commit adultery; and whoever marries a divorced woman commits adultery."*

Matthew 5:32 [emphasis added]

> *"And I say to you, whoever divorces his wife, **except for immorality**, and marries another woman commits adultery."*

Matthew 19:9 [emphasis added]

We have noted multiple times already that divorce is never banned in the Scriptures, only regulated. However, in his regulations, Moses never gave specific grounds for divorce that can or should be considered acceptable. The husband just had to find something that caused his wife to lose his favor (see Deuteronomy 24:1-4). In Matthew, Jesus actually gave specific allowable grounds for divorce where both partners are Christians – "unchastity" (5:32) or "immorality" (19:9).[1]

It would do us well to do a little bit of word study before we continue. In most conservative churches, we are taught that *adultery* is the only acceptable grounds for divorce. So the words "adultery" and "unchastity" (and "immorality"; "fornication", KJV) are treated as synonyms, when in reality they are not. (We will look at adultery in more detail in the next section.) Without getting into a lot of linguistic detail, we will do just enough word study here to get the basis for the current discussion.

A quick look at the Greek New Testament gives an interesting discovery: the English words "unchastity", "immorality", and "fornication" are all translated from the same Greek noun, *porneia*.[2] In most Greek literature,

---

[1] Do not forget that Jesus' teachings in Matthew, supported by Paul in 1 Corinthians 7, are applicable today for Christians *only*. Marriages where one or both of the partners is unsaved do not fall within the scope of this chapter. See the previous chapter for that discussion.

[2] Our English word "pornography" comes from a combination of the Greek *porneia* ("illicit sexuality") and *graphē* ("a writing"). Pornography is nothing more than written (and now recorded on audio and video as well) sexual perversity.

107

including the New Testament, *porneia* is used as a "catch-all" word to include every sort of sexual impurity. In addition to general promiscuity, it is also used in reference to adultery, homosexuality, sodomy, bestiality, premarital sexuality, and any other form of non-marital sex.

To understand this meaning in Jesus' teaching (based on what His immediate listeners understood), God allows two married Christians to divorce if one of the partners is sexually unfaithful to the other.

I do have to make another point here about the strict interpretation of Jesus words. During the time in which Jesus lived, women were often considered to be property of their fathers or husbands more than individual people. This is why both Moses and Jesus refer to the husband divorcing his wife, and not the other way around. Ironside and most others take this one step beyond what is strictly stated in the text. He believes that for today, whichever mate was faithful can file for divorce instead of just the husband (see Mark 10:11-12).

> The clear sense of this passage is evident. The adulterous husband or wife breaks the tie. A divorce in the courts legalizes the separation, and the inno-

cent one is as free before God as though never married at all.[3]

## Only Sexual Unfaithfulness?

Wayne and Amanda[4] were married three years ago last month. Their son, Jeremy, is 10 months old. For the most part, things have gone reasonably well. Things happened shortly after the wedding that they had not expected, but nothing really major or anything they could not handle together. From all appearances, they were a happy couple. But something, somewhere, fell apart. Wayne became continually abusive with his words in the home. His attitude forced guilt on Amanda whenever she tried to bring it up. The mouth that once spoke the vows of the covenant and said "I love you" was now filled with words of hatred and resentment or nothing at all. There

---

[3] H. A. Ironside, *Expository Notes on the Gospel of Matthew* (New York: Loizeaux, 1948), p. 53.

[4] This couple and all details are completely fictional. I do not have anyone in mind as I write. However, in reality this happens all too frequently and gives us a good basis upon which to commence this final discussion on divorce.

was no sexual affair, but the hurt was just as bad, if not worse. She had had enough; she filed for divorce. How sad. How tragic. How can something that was so wonderful at the beginning end in such a mess?

Though we would much rather not think about it, the reason for this section is not hard to figure out. Most Christians agree that sexual unfaithfulness is sufficient grounds for divorce. But what about cases of abuse, neglect, or physical harm? What option is there for those women who are truly afraid to be alone with their husbands or vice versa? Is divorce a biblical option, or must they suffer through each hour, hoping, praying that their spouses would actually have an affair so they could file for a divorce on the biblical ground of sexual unfaithfulness?

In order to help you understand the line of reasoning here, let me share with you Jay Adams' explanation of *adultery*:

> The interesting fact about the word *adultery* is that it has reference always to more than sexual sin. The marriage covenant is always in view. In addition to the notion of sexual unfaithfulness, adultery refers to the violation of the covenant of companionship by the introduction of another party into the picture. This third party appears on the

> scene in order to provide companion-
> ship (usually, if not always, of a sexual
> nature) instead of the wife or husband
> "of one's youth."[5] [italics original]

Notice that it is not necessarily a sexual affair. Though it is primarily associated with extra-marital sex (and rightly so), adultery must not be confused with the sex act itself, because it may include anything that violates that covenant of companionship between the marriage partners. In fact, the word "adultery" is used figuratively throughout the Bible to mean unfaithfulness in general, not just physical unfaithfulness.[6]

> Idolatry, covetousness, and apostasy are
> spoken of as adultery spiritually (Jer.
> 3:6, 8, 9; Ezek. 16:32; Hos. 1, 2, 3 Rev.
> 2:22). An apostate church is an adulte-
> ress (Isa. 1:21; Ezek. 23:4, 7, 37), and the
> Jews are styled "an adulterous genera-
> tion" (Matt. 12:39). (Compare Rev. 12.)[7]

---

[5] Adams, p. 54.

[6] In the Old Testament prophets, see Jeremiah 3:9; 5:7; Ezekiel 23:37, 43; Hosea 2:2. In the New Testament both Jesus and Peter taught that adultery was a heart sin, not just a sex sin; see Matthew 5:28 and 2 Peter 2:14.

[7] *Easton's Bible Dictionary*, electronic edition, "adultery".

> Jesus' teachings expanded the Old Tes-
> tament law to address matters of the
> heart. Adultery has its origins within
> (Matt. 15:19), and lust is as much a vi-
> olation of the law's intent as is illicit
> sexual intercourse (Matt. 5:27-28). Adul-
> tery is one of the "works of the flesh"
> (Gal. 5:19). It creates enmity with God
> (Jas. 4:4), and adulterers will not inherit
> the kingdom of God (1 Cor. 6:9).[8]

Now, I understand that one of my major
points in the previous section is that "adultery"
cannot be used interchangeably with "unchastity", "immorality", or "fornication", which is
the only ground for divorce which Jesus
specifies. However, again, we must be careful
to never take all of our doctrine from only one
or two phrases when there are others available
with which we can compare our text in question. Remember that Jesus did not set out to
make a once and for all doctrine of divorce. He
did not even introduce the subject; it was
brought to Him. His statements in Matthew
19:3-9 are direct answers to direct questions

---

[8] *Holman Bible Dictionary*, "adultery",
www.studylight.org; accessed 12/13/2006.

asked of Him.[9]  Given His short, direct answers and lack of continued teaching on the subject, we must conclude that this was not meant to be His full answer for every aspect of this subject.

## Christian Discipline

The Bible is very clear regarding the framework and procedure under which Christians are to be disciplined when they are unrepentant for their sin.  We have already seen that divorce is simply an alternative, not a command, when one partner has violated the marital covenant.  Reconciliation is by far the best option.  But what happens when the partner's sin is not sexual infidelity and he or she is still unrepentant, as in the case of ongoing physical or verbal abuse?  Can a divorce be biblically-grounded under these circumstances?

Let's look at the progressive steps of Christian discipline outlined in Scripture (Matthew 18:15-17).

---

[9] Refresh your memory of the passage in question by re-reading chapter six if you need to before continuing here.

## First, *confront the sinning brother*[10] *in love*

> *"If your brother sins, go and show him*
> *his fault in private; if he listens to you,*
> *you have won your brother."* (vs. 15)

## Secondly, *confront him again with witnesses*

> *"But if he does not listen to you, take*
> *one or two more with you, so that BY*
> *THE MOUTH OF TWO OR THREE WIT-*
> *NESSES EVERY FACT MAY BE CON-*
> *FIRMED."* (vs. 16)

## Thirdly, *take the matter before the elders of the local church*[11]

---

[10] The term "brother" in these steps and passages refers to all Christians, whether male or female. In the interest of simplicity, I will not use "brother / sister" and "his / her" for each of these points.

[11] The reason for the elders rather than the whole congregation directly is because of the spiritual authority and leadership the elders hold in the assembly, in this case to make the judgment on whether the matter is serious enough to have the congregation enforce the next step. It is unthinkable that Jesus would be teaching that any church member can bring any other church member before the congregation for discipline without going through the divinely-ordered spiritual leadership of the assembly. As with many other parts of this study,

*"If he refuses to listen to them, tell it to the church;"* (vs. 17a)

Fourthly, *consider and treat the sinning brother as an unbeliever*

> *"and if he refuses to listen even to the church, let him be to you as a Gentile and a tax collector."* (vs. 17b)

Remember our hypothetical case? Both partners profess to be Christians, and at one point they were both living their lives in accordance with God's will. This would include membership in a local church. Now one of them is in sin, but it is not sexual immorality. The offended partner wants out of the "relationship" (with assumed good reason), but since the sin is not sexual in nature, the

---

this passage must be considered alongside other passages before making doctrinal convictions. This was only the second mention of the church in the entire Bible (see Matthew 16:18 for the first). This is not the last word on church discipline in the New Testament, especially since the church was not even established at this point (see 1 Corinthians 5:1-5; 2 Corinthians 2:5-11).

case is not mentioned specifically in Scripture. What is the solution?

If indeed the sinning partner is a member of a local church and is unrepentant, then the above steps *must* be followed. The purpose of all true discipline, of course, is repentance and restoration (see Galatians 6:1). If that never happens then we must consider the results of the final disciplinary step.

At this time I feel it necessary to raise a point about how Christians may and may not conduct affairs with other Christians. Specifically in reference to judicial matters, Paul says,

> [1]*When one of you has a dispute with another believer, how dare you file a lawsuit and ask a secular court to decide the matter instead of taking it to other believers!* [2]*Don't you realize that someday we believers will judge the world? And since you are going to judge the world, can't you decide even these little things among yourselves?* [3]*Don't you realize that we will judge angels? So you should surely be able to resolve ordinary disputes in this life.* [4]*If you have legal disputes about such matters, why go to outside judges who are not respected by the church?* [5]*I am saying this to shame you. Isn't there anyone in all the church who is wise enough to decide these issues?* [6]*But instead, one believer sues another-- right in front of unbelievers!*

> *7Even to have such lawsuits with one another is a defeat for you. Why not just accept the injustice and leave it at that? Why not let yourselves be cheated? 8Instead, you yourselves are the ones who do wrong and cheat even your fellow believers.*

1 Corinthians 6:1-8 (NLT)

Simply stated, Christians are not to take each other to court.  Ever.  If there are matters that cannot be worked out between Christians directly, the elders of the church, not attorneys, should be approached to solve them.  In matters of marriage, Christian partners *must not* take each other to divorce court.  How, then, can a divorce be obtained if both partners are Christians?  This is where the disciplinary process enters.

In reference to the question about two Christians divorcing based on the sexual immorality of one of the partners, Chuck Swindoll says,

> When a spouse is guilty of immoral sexual conduct with another person and is unwilling to remain faithful to the innocent partner, the option is there for the faithful mate to divorce and remarry... But there are occasions when every attempt has been made to keep the marriage together...but sustained sexual infidelity won't allow it.  It is in such cases our Lord grants freedom [Mat-

117

thew 19:9] from that miserable and unbearable bond.[12]


If the disciplinary steps in Matthew
18:15-17 are followed and the sinning partner
refuses to repent somewhere during the
process, but instead continues in his/her
current pattern of unfaithfulness to the marriage vows, that partner is to be considered by
Christians to be an unbeliever.[13] This would
automatically create a mixed marriage between
the two. At this point, after excommunication
from the local assembly, should that partner
still refuse to repent and continues the pattern
of sin, the offended partner has just as much
right to divorce as one who is married to
someone who never claimed salvation at all.

A stretch, you think? If so, then how
much force do you really think your vows
hold? Consider what I say when performing a

---

[12] Swindoll, pp. 15-16.

[13] The phrase "as a Gentile and a tax collector" in verse
17 is picturesque. At this time in history, Gentiles were
not yet a part of the covenant. Tax collectors, though
Jews, were traitors, unfaithfully selling out their own
people for personal gain. The analogy must not be lost
to a marriage partner who has "sold out" the other
spouse through unfaithfulness.

wedding where the couple has chosen to use
the standard marriage vows:

> These vows which you are about to
> make to each other are lasting vows be-
> fore God and these witnesses. In Eccle-
> siastes 5:5, Solomon warns us "It is
> better that you should not vow than that
> you should vow and not pay."

> Do you, *[Groom]*,
> take this woman to be your wedded
> wife,
> to love and respect her,
> to honor and cherish her,
> for better or for worse,
> for richer or for poorer,
> in sickness and in health,
> and leaving all others to keep yourself
> only to her, so long as you both shall
> live?

> [The bride then follows with the same
> vows to him, with little, if any, differ-
> ence.]

We often quote the last half of the vows,
while we just as often neglect the third and
fourth lines. When my wife and I were married, I vowed to her that I would "love and
respect her" as well as "honor and cherish

her…as long as [we] both shall live". Is it not obvious that sexual infidelity is not the only way to break this covenant?

We have already seen that in the Sermon on the Mount, Jesus added our heart actions to the physical actions that could break the Law and its intent. We also recognize that, as in many other teachings, Jesus did not necessarily mean to finalize the discussion with His exception. So it may very well be true that "adultery" (or unfaithfulness) of any sort can be acceptable grounds for a biblical divorce, if the process for Christian discipline is followed all the way through to its biblical conclusion. The problem is that this discipline is rare in even solid, Bible-preaching churches today. What a disservice to those who would gladly repent if they were simply confronted about their sin. The disservice also extends to the faithful spouse who is never released from this "miserable and unbearable bond" because God's pattern for discipline is not followed.

## The Responsibility of the Local Church

This last section is related to how Christians deal with people who have divorces in their past. Though we will discuss the aspects of local church offices and more formal details later, I feel that it is important to close this section with a final word on the effect of divorce on the character of those who have been through it.

As I alluded in the introduction to this study, divorce is too often regarded, though not usually outright said, to be an "unpardonable sin". With our "holier-than-thou" attitudes, we Christians who have never had to tread the path of divorce have incessantly looked down on those who have with nothing less than contempt, judging them to be "second-class Christians" because of their unfortunate past. Can we really find defense for this disgusting action in God's Word, much less His very nature?

Since he has done so well already, I find no need to say any more, but rather quote Chuck Swindoll here. Though he specifies a marriage and divorce that occurred before salvation, the principle to which he refers can obviously be applied after salvation as well (see 1 John 1:9). Here is Ephesians 2:1-7 and 19-22, then Swindoll's earnest observation on these verses:

> ¹*And you were dead in your trespasses and sins, ²in which you formerly walked according to the course of this world,*

*according to the prince of the power of the air, of the spirit that is now working in the sons of disobedience. [3]Among them we too all formerly lived in the lusts of our flesh, indulging the desires of the flesh and of the mind, and were by nature children of wrath, even as the rest. [4]But God, being rich in mercy, because of His great love with which He loved us, [5]even when we were dead in our transgressions, made us alive together with Christ (by grace you have been saved), [6]and raised us up with Him, and seated us with Him in the heavenly places in Christ Jesus, [7]so that in the ages to come He might show the surpassing riches of His grace in kindness toward us in Christ Jesus...*

*[19]So then you are no longer strangers and aliens, but you are fellow citizens with the saints, and are of God's household, [20]having been built on the foundation of the apostles and prophets, Christ Jesus Himself being the corner stone, [21]in whom the whole building, being fitted together, is growing into a holy temple in the Lord, [22]in whom you also are being built together into a dwelling of God in the Spirit.*

Quite frankly, it is beyond my comprehension that passages such as these (there are dozens more) exclude divorce. If they do, then divorce is the only sin not covered by the blood of Christ. It is the one, permanent spot in our past that cannot be washed away. Furthermore, it is then questionable that we can take the words of David at face value when he writes

*He has not dealt with us according to our sins,*

*Nor rewarded us according to our iniquities.*

*For as high as the heavens are above the earth,*

*So great is His lovingkindness toward those who fear Him.*

*As far as the east is from the west,*

*So far has He removed our transgressions from us. (Psalm 103:10-12)*

...Having thought through this very carefully, I believe it falls within the context of God's superabundant grace to wipe our slate clean when we turn, by faith, to Christ the Lord.[14]

---

[14] Swindoll, p. 12.

# PART THREE

# REMARRIAGE

# CHAPTER NINE
## THE CASE FOR REMARRIAGE

As we begin this last part of our study, there are two final discussions to be tackled, each with its own full set of questions and answers: 1) *When, if ever, is remarriage acceptable?* and 2) *How is remarriage to be handled in the local church?* We will devote the next two chapters to the first question and the concluding chapter to the other.

By its own concession, "remarriage" is simply marrying again. Since a person cannot remarry if he or she had not been married previously, remarriage can be considered in only two scenarios: death or divorce. Let us first examine remarriage after the death of a spouse.

## Remarriage Allowed

There probably is not an easier place to start (if we can call anything on this subject "easy") than where remarriage is clearly allowed with only a few restrictions. As we have noted before, even though Paul is not focusing on our subject directly in Romans 7, since he uses it as an example, we are allowed to glean principles that are applicable. Again we turn to Romans 7:1-3:

> [1]*Or do you not know, brethren (for I am speaking to those who know the law), that the law has jurisdiction over a person as long as he lives?* [2]*For the married woman is bound by law to her husband while he is living; but if her husband dies, she is released from the law concerning the husband.* [3]*So then, if while her husband is living she is joined to another man, she shall be called an adulteress; but if her husband dies, she is free from the law, so that she is not an adulteress though she is joined to another man.*

I'm not sure how Paul could make it any clearer than this: once a marriage partner dies, the surviving mate is completely free to remarry. The widow or widower cannot be called an adulteress or adulterer because the marriage covenant was not breached; it was actually made null and void at the death of one of the covenanters. All marital obligations cease to exist toward the dead spouse. The survivor is "released" and "free" to be "joined to another". He repeats this teaching at the end of his thesis on the subject in 1 Corinthians 7:39.

> *"A wife is bound as long as her husband lives; but if her husband is dead, **she is free to be married to whom she wishes**, only in the Lord."* [emphasis added]

The only restriction that we can find in Scripture toward a remarriage (in this instance) is that if the surviving partner is a Christian, he or she is not to marry an unbeliever ("only in the Lord"). Other than this, there are no restrictions on a remarriage for a widow(er).

## Remarriage Urged

As we continue toward the more complex remarriage situations, the next "easiest" passage to explore must be 1 Timothy 5:14. Here we find Paul giving a definite plea for women who were widowed early in life to be remarried:

> *Therefore, **I want younger widows to get***
> ***married**, bear children, keep house, and give*
> *the enemy no occasion for reproach;* [emphasis added]

The Greek word translated "I want" means "to plan on a course of action".[1] Paul stopped just short of commanding younger widows to remarry.

We have just seen in Romans 7:1-3 that God clearly allows for remarriage after a spouse's death, though He did not command it. This being the understanding, why would Paul go as far as making a plea for certain widows to remarry? Apparently, there is a definite purpose that Paul has in mind as he makes this desire known. To understand his reasoning, we must look at the context surrounding our immediate passage:

> [11]*But refuse to put younger widows on the*
> *list, for when they feel sensual desires in dis-*
> *regard of Christ, they want to get married,*
> [12]*thus incurring condemnation, because*
> *they have set aside their previous pledge.*
> [13]*At the same time they also learn to be idle,*
> *as they go around from house to house; and*
> *not merely idle, but also gossips and busy-*
> *bodies, talking about things not proper to*

---

[1] BDAG, *boulomai.*

> *mention. [14]Therefore, I want younger wi-*
> *dows to get married, bear children, keep*
> *house, and give the enemy no occasion for*
> *reproach; [15]for some have already turned*
> *aside to follow Satan.*

1 Timothy 5:11-15

In the previous verses we find Paul telling Timothy to keep a list of widows who have no family to support them. If these widows (called "widows indeed", vs. 3) have met certain qualifications, the church is to support them, possibly in remuneration for services and ministries being performed by them in the church.[2] However, Paul takes special note of those women whose husbands died early, leaving them alone at a young age. In addition to these women having not yet met the qualifications to be considered "widows indeed", Paul has other concerns about young widows.

First, *they may want to marry again in the future (vs. 11-12).* As we shall see in chapter eleven, widows indeed apparently were re-quired to make a vow ("their previous pledge", vs. 12) to spend the remainder of their lives in the service of the church, never remar-

---

[2] We will consider this position of "widow indeed" in more detail in Chapter 11.

rying.[3]  Because of the gravity with which God approaches vows made to Him (Ecclesiastes 5:5), Paul did not want these young women committing themselves to God, only to burn with "sensual desires" that are to be fulfilled only in marriage and put themselves into a position where their hearts and minds, though promised to God, cannot be wholly His.  A remarriage in this case, though allowing them acceptable sexual fulfillment, would break their vow to God.  He refers to these "desires" in our main Corinthians passage as well.

> *[8]But I say to the unmarried and to widows that it is good for them if they remain even as I. [9]But if they do not have self-control, let them marry; for it is better to marry than to burn with passion.*

> 1 Corinthians 7:8-9 [emphasis added]

Apparently some were trying to be "holy" or "devoted to God" by remaining celibate, but they just could not get past their (God-given, by the way) desire for sex.  Note

---

[3] A pre-church age example of a young widow making this type of vow may be the "prophetess" Anna in Luke 2:36-37, who was widowed after only seven years of marriage and did not remarry.

that he includes those who have not yet married as well as those who have lost a spouse. He did not say that all remarriage is bad. In fact, he urged them to not continue putting themselves into a position where they not only "burn with passion", but also where those passions may lead them into sexual sin if they were not satisfied according to God's plan.

Paul's second concern was that *their singleness may lead them into sin (vs. 13-15)*. While this is not meant to be an insult to women (because it can apply to men also, see 2 Thessalonians 3:11-12), the concern is that if the young women have nothing to do (in regard to raising a family or keeping a full house), they would fall into the sins of idleness, gossip, and busybodiness. Though the adage is not found in Scripture directly, the principle definitely is that "idle hands are the Devil's workshop." Paul said that not only would Satan have reason to "reproach" these women (and then the church at large), but that some had actually "turned aside to follow" him.

The principle is not hard to miss: since God created humans to marry, to not do so (even after being widowed) could cause avoidable problems, both in the personal lives of the widows and the life of the local assembly.

# CHAPTER TEN
## BIBLICAL REMARRIAGE AFTER DIVORCE?

We have established that God created marriage to be permanent *for life*. But what about after divorce? Since marriage was created to be permanent, is that couple, though legally divorced, still married in God's sight? In other words, does God recognize human divorce? While remarriage after death is considered to be worthy, those (Christians and non-Christians alike) who remarry after divorce are often treated by church members with disdain. A primary reason is because of a phrase which clouds this whole issue, especially among Christians – "in God's sight".

There are only two ways to find out what someone thinks or believes to be true. The first is to become that person, enter into his mind and read his exact thoughts. Of course, this is humanly impossible. The second way, however, is not. This is done simply by listening to that person as he explains what he believes on any given topic, such as what you are doing with my own thoughts and convictions while you read this book. While we accept this way of understanding each other to be true in relation to other humans, for some reason we think that it stops short of applying to God. Even Christians will attempt to make God say something that He does not mean by scouring the Bible for "deeper meanings" behind the literal text. But to understand marriage, divorce, or remarriage "in God's sight", all we really need to do is read His mind as He gave it to us on paper. So once again we turn to Scripture in order to find His teaching and form our beliefs.

## Proper Remarriages

We have noted that when Moses established the regulations on divorce in Deuteronomy 24:1-4, it was because those divorces were already occurring on an apparently regular basis. A look at the passage again shows that the same holds true for remarriage as well.

> *[1]When a man takes a wife and marries her,
> and it happens that she finds no favor in his
> eyes because he has found some indecency in*

> her, and he writes her a certificate of divorce
> and puts it in her hand and sends her out
> from his house, ²and she leaves his house
> and goes and becomes another man's wife,
> ³and if the latter husband turns against her
> and writes her a certificate of divorce and
> puts it in her hand and sends her out of his
> house, or if the latter husband dies who took
> her to be his wife, ⁴then her former husband
> who sent her away is not allowed to take her
> again to be his wife, since she has been de-
> filed; for that is an abomination before the
> LORD, and you shall not bring sin on the
> land which the LORD your God gives you
> as an inheritance.

As we dissected this passage with divorce in mind, I found something that was conspicuously missing: guidelines for remarriage. The only regulation on remarriage was that a divorced couple could not be reconciled in marriage if another marriage had already taken place. While giving all of the information about divorce, Moses seemed to deliberately dismiss remarriage as being a problem. The attitude was that once the divorce was final and legalized, all obligations of that marriage covenant were null and void and another covenant could commence. Matthew Henry puts it this way:

> That being divorced it was lawful for
> her to marry another husband, v. 2. The
> divorce had dissolved the bond of mar-

riage as effectually as death could dissolve it; so that she was as free to marry again as if her first husband had been naturally dead.[1]

We find the same to be true in the comments of both Jesus and Paul. Consider these passages again.

> [31]*It was said, "WHOEVER SENDS HIS WIFE AWAY, LET HIM GIVE HER A CERTIFICATE OF DIVORCE"; [32]but I say to you that everyone who divorces his wife, except for the reason of unchastity, makes her commit adultery; and whoever marries a divorced woman commits adultery.*

Matthew 5:31-32

> [8]*He said to them, "Because of your hardness of heart Moses permitted you to divorce your wives; but from the beginning it has not been this way. [9]And I say to you, whoever divorces his wife, except for immorality, and marries another woman commits adultery."*

Matthew 19:8-9

> *Yet if the unbelieving one leaves, let him leave; the brother or the sister is not under*

---

[1] Henry, p. 266.

*bondage in such cases, but God has called us
to peace.*

1 Corinthians 7:15

Up to this point we have focused specifically on divorce in these passages. We understand that Jesus' comments were direct
answers to direct questions about divorce. In
the context Jesus had rebuked the Jews for
taking liberties with the Scriptures, resulting in
improper divorces that fell outside of the
biblical guidelines. His comments on remarriage, then, must be understood in the light of
improper divorce. When He said "whoever
marries a divorced woman commits adultery",
He was specifically referencing those who
remarry after an unbiblical, or improper,
divorce. He does not, however, mention
remarriage after a proper divorce because that
was not a part of the discussion at hand. We
must assume, then, that the converse of His
statements will hold true. If remarriage is
improper after an *improper divorce*, then we can
assume (since it is not told us otherwise) that a
remarriage is proper after a *proper divorce*.

Paul supports this understanding of
Jesus' words. He said that in the case of a

proper divorce between a believer and an unbeliever, the believer "is not under bondage". The word "bondage" reminds us of Romans 7:2 where Paul tells us that married couples are "bound by law". In his example, when a marriage partner dies, the survivor is "released" and "free" to be "joined to another". This teaching is the same in 1 Corinthians 7:15 where the believer "is not under bondage" when the divorce is done according to the biblical regulations. This "bondage" refers to the marriage covenant. When a divorce is secured according to the biblical regulations, the marriage covenant is voided, allowing the ex-partners to enter into a new, biblical covenant.

In addition to chapters six and eight of this book and the Bible passages already given which deal with this question, let us look at one more statement by Paul for a final answer to this issue.

> *27Are you bound to a wife? Do not seek to be released. Are you released from a wife? Do not seek a wife. 28But if you marry, you have not sinned;*

> 1 Corinthians 7:27-28a

Even those who believe that the passages above should not be applied to remarriage after divorce situations cannot ignore these verses. Paul uses the same idea of "bound" and "released" as before, but (I believe, in order to clarify) he goes one step further; spousal death cannot be applied here. "Do not seek to be released." Is Paul saying, "Do not pray for God to take your wife."? Or, "Do not look for a way to kill your husband."? *Of course not!* This can apply to divorce only. "If you are married, do not look for a reason to divorce." *But* in those cases where a proper divorce has occurred ("Are you released..."), "if you marry, you have not sinned."[2] Coming fresh off of the instructions for a proper divorce, Paul's meaning cannot be made any clearer: *remarriage after a proper divorce is legitimate and proper.*

What about "in God's sight"? Weren't these two to be married until death? Yes, that was God's intention. But remember John R. W. Stott's discerning comment on divorce, that it is "a divine concession to human weakness." An understanding of the whole of God's grace shows us nothing less. Our salvation, at its

---

[2] The two questions *have* to refer to the same thing for the contrast to get its intended effect. If the first "release" is referring to divorce rather than death, the second "release" must as well.

most basic level, is God yielding to the fact that when He allowed us to have a free will, He allowed us to choose evil as well as good. Though His perfect will was that we would choose good, He did indeed want us to choose.[3] We chose poorly. He compensated, or made "concession", by offering us something which cost Him dearly – His Son's life. We do not have to search for God's intended plan for marriage in man's divorce. Nor do we have to try to line up man's divorce within God's plan for marriage, because it is not there. However, in His concession, He does indeed recognize mankind's divorces as valid "in His sight", as long as the divorce is done according to His stated regulations. So when the marriage covenant is voided, whether by death or proper divorce, each individual person is free to enter a new marriage covenant with another person, so long as that new covenant follows His guidelines as well ("free to be married…in the Lord", 1 Corinthians 7:39).

---

[3] C. S. Lewis offers a thought-provoking discussion regarding God's sovereignty in conjunction with man's free will in his classic *Mere Christianity*, in the chapter entitled "The Shocking Alternative".

## Improper Remarriages

You cannot read the above section without noticing that almost every time I mention divorce, I clarify it by some form of the word "proper". Simple deductive reasoning, then, says that if proper divorces can yield proper remarriages, then improper divorces must yield improper remarriages. The question then is this: what constitutes an improper divorce when remarriage should not be considered?

In order to determine what makes an *improper* divorce, we must first review what makes a *proper* divorce. The guidelines are as follows:

1. In mixed marriages, divorce is acceptable only if the unbelieving spouse leaves by breaking the covenant. If so, "the brother or sister is not under bondage in such cases" (1 Corinthians 7:15)

2. In Christian marriages:

   a. If one partner commits sexual immorality, the marriage covenant is broken and divorce is allowed as an option (Matthew 5:32; 19:9). However, reconciliation through repentance and forgiveness is preferred. Christian discipline should be observed to bring the sinning spouse to this point.

b. If one partner breaks the marriage covenant by something other than sexual immorality, the Christian discipline steps are to be taken, for the purpose of repentance, forgiveness, and reconciliation (Matthew 18:15-17; 1 Corinthians 5:1-5; 2 Corinthians 2:5-11). If, after the confrontations, the Christian is still unrepentant and continues to live in a pattern of sin, that partner is to be excommunicated and considered to be the same as an unbeliever. At this point a mixed marriage is in effect. If repentance still does not follow, the process for divorce in a mixed marriage applies.

Since these are the only occasions for proper divorce that the Bible provides, anything else *must* be considered improper. Since the possible real situations are too numerous to list here (and I would probably miss many anyway), let's return to our hypothetical couple from chapter eight, Wayne and Amanda. However, instead of Wayne being the one completely in the wrong with verbal and emotional abuse, let's just say that the two were constantly fighting. They could not agree on anything. Somehow they had grown apart in those three years, and their fights were never-ending. Instead of going to their pastor or church counselors, they decided to simply divorce on the grounds of "incompatibility". Since they were having problems at home, they had stopped attending church, because they did not want to have to pretend that everything was okay. In the meantime, Wayne meets Laura, a nice Christian woman, and begins to date her and attend her church. He does not hide from her that he is divorced. Soon they want to be married, and so they approach the pastor of their church. What should be the pastor's response to their request for marriage?

Based on what we have learned in this study, we find many things that should have happened but did not. At this point, the only acceptable solution is the following:

1. "Incompatibility" is not found in the New Testament as acceptable grounds for divorce. So the divorce is *improper*, and Wayne and Amanda are still bound by their marriage covenant, making a remarriage also improper.

2. Had the pastors or elders of Wayne and Amanda's church been correctly fulfilling their responsibility of shepherding, they would have intervened well before the divorce was finalized, hopefully before the divorce attorney was hired. Since they did not, the steps of Christian discipline (which may have brought about marital reconciliation) were not observed.

3. Since Amanda has not yet remarried, there are only two correct courses of action:

   a. Wayne and Amanda should be counseled by a pastor (preferably the former pastor who already knows them) to reconcile their marriage, even though they are already divorced, because the divorce was not proper. Reconciliation happens through the process of repentance (on both sides) and forgiveness (from both sides). Remarriage to each other, then, is the correction of their divorce.

b. Should one of them not repent, Christian discipline must proceed, ultimately clearing them of all obligations to each other, making their formerly improper divorce, proper.

Obviously, there are many things that could make this more complicated than I have done here. What if Amanda had remarried already? What if Wayne and Laura married, then Amanda, who did not marry, wanted to reconcile her marriage to Wayne? Since he was already remarried, where would that leave her? Because this book cannot solve every specific problem, I must leave those questions to the pastors and elders who will be working with them directly. However, not one of these situations is irresolvable when approached with a clear understanding of God's Word. The more complicated situations simply increase the time and effort it takes to resolve them. However, God never leaves us without a resolution. His written Word is sufficient for every problem which we create.

# CHAPTER ELEVEN
# DIVORCE AND REMARRIAGE IN THE CHURCH

This chapter is probably where many people will disagree with me (even those who have not already done so). These questions are doubtless the most difficult to answer when dealing with a Christian who has been divorced: How is divorce and remarriage to be handled in the local church? What are the biblical guidelines for accepting this person into (or back into) the assembly? How can this person be used in the church? In what ministries can he or she serve? We will attempt to answer all of these in this final chapter of our study.

## The Situation

Many times individuals wanting to remarry will seek the counsel of a pastor (usually of a different church than they may have been attending) before making that decision. What they *ask* is, "Will you marry us?". What they are *really asking* is, "How will your church receive us?". Some pastors will refuse remarriage completely. Others will allow remarriage only if the former partner is deceased. Still others will allow remarriage in any case.

Does the reason for the divorce make a difference in recommending or not recommending remarriage? *Absolutely!* Armed with the information we have found in our study, a good pastor will dig into the circumstances and proceedings of the divorce to make sure that it was done properly and that there are no outstanding obligations prohibiting a proper remarriage. Unfortunately, there are many churches that will not accept divorcees, much less those who have remarried, into their membership. Even if the couple *is* granted membership, the congregation may treat them as strangers or outsiders.

In many cases where a church does accept them into membership, however, hospitality is not the problem. The people welcome them with open arms and love them. The recurring problem is that of service. A lot of churches today still will not allow a divorced person or remarried divorcees to be involved in the Christian service of the local church. For some reason they no longer see these people, who have suffered through these problems, as qualified to serve God in certain areas. Things are said like, "Well, you can serve as custodian, but you'll not teach." Or, "You may teach the children, but those with a divorce in their past cannot teach other adults." This attitude, above all others, causes many persons and couples to move from church to church and finally stop attending church altogether because they are not allowed to serve. They become discouraged by the resistance and decide that it is not worth the effort to continue. It upsets me to think of the number of downtrodden Christians who want nothing but to continue their lives in service for God but are unable to do so because churches do not observe and obey God's Word on divorce and remarriage.

In the final section of chapter eight we touched on how God views repentant people in these situations – they are sinners, saved by

His grace (Ephesians 2:8-9); forgiven of their sin (1 John 1:9; 2 Corinthians 2:5-11); specially ordained to do good works of service (Ephesians 2:10); spiritually gifted by God for the edification of other believers (1 Corinthians 12:7); and capable of growing in spiritual maturity and serving Him with the remainder of their lives (1 Corinthians 6:11). Let's see how we can put this attitude into action in our own assemblies.

## Elders and Deacons

God gave the qualifications for elders and deacons in two places: 1 Timothy 3:1-13 and Titus 1:5-9. In both of these passages we find the phrase "the husband of one wife" (elders – 1 Timothy 3:2, Titus 1:6; deacons – 1 Timothy 3:12). What does that mean?

The Greek phrase used in all three of these verses, literally translated, is "a one-woman man". Across denominations, and even within denominations, this phrase is widely misunderstood and debated. There are five main interpretations, however, and each one is important to take into consideration.[1]

## Exclusion of unmarried men

Though there are not many who hold to this, Oliver Greene's comments summarize their view adequately:

> It is my conviction that a man placed in the office of bishop, deacon – or in the capacity of leadership, regardless of the title of the office – should be a married man, a man who has only one living wife.[2]

From the numerous objections to this view, allow me to share two. First, had Paul meant for unmarried men to be excluded from this office he would have said "husband of *a* wife" rather than using the numeral "one". Secondly, this interpretation of Paul's grammar would also require elders and deacons to have

---

[1] This list was adapted from John Hartog II, *The Biblical Qualifications of a Pastor* (Columbus, GA: Brentwood Christian Press, 1992), pp. 23-28.

[2] Oliver B. Greene, *The Epistles of Paul the Apostle to Timothy and Titus* (Greenville, SC: The Gospel Hour, 1964), pp. 108-109.

two or more children as well, because of the qualifications "keeping his children under control" and "good managers of *their* children (vs. 1 Timothy 3:4, 12).

### Prohibition of remarried widowers

The proponents of this view teach that if the elder or deacon is a widower, he may never remarry, taking "one wife" to an extreme. Since I have already shown the Bible support for remarriage after the death of a spouse (see chapter nine), I will not spend any more time on it here.

### Prohibition of divorce

While the first three views are obviously incorrect and should be avoided, these last three are often debated, each with a wealth of supporting arguments by its advocates. Those who support this fourth teaching believe that Paul's requirement means that elders and deacons may never have been divorced, even before their salvation. Some go as far as to teach that their wives must also have no history of divorce. Their main argument is that, while God can forgive these men for being divorced, the consequences of their divorces prohibit them from such high offices as elder and deacon.

The primary objection to this teaching is that it assumes all divorce to be wrong. While it is true that even proper divorces (as we have defined them in this study) may have consequences, the Bible never (unless these verses are the only exception) eliminates Christians from service based on their sinful pasts. In fact Paul told the Corinthians

> *⁹Or do you not know that the unrighteous will not inherit the kingdom of God? Do not be deceived; neither fornicators, nor idolaters, nor adulterers, nor effeminate, nor homosexuals, ¹⁰nor thieves, nor the covetous, nor drunkards, nor revilers, nor swindlers, will inherit the kingdom of God. ¹¹Such were some of you; but you were washed, but you were sanctified, but you were justified in the name of the Lord Jesus Christ and in the Spirit of our God.*
>
> 1 Corinthians 6:8-11

Look at this list of what we would consider horrible sins and crimes. Yet Paul was able to say "such were some of you". These Christians had more-than-checkered pasts, but they had been forgiven and "justified". To be justified means to be declared righteous by God. If people with these sins in their pasts could be declared righteous and acceptable for service to God, why should those with *proper* divorces not be considered the same?[3] Especially since divorce isn't even considered bad enough to include in this list?

## Prohibition of polygamy

Those who support this second most-discussed teaching take the phrase to mean that elders and deacons must have "only one wife at a time". An advocate of this view, Jay Adams spends two pages in his book, *Marriage, Divorce, and Remarriage in the Bible*, giving supporting arguments for his case.[4] He gives historical support from both classical Greek and Roman writings, as well as from the Jewish historian, Josephus, regarding the abundance of polygamous relationships among the Jews at the time of Paul's writing and later.

---

[3] Paul spends three chapters (12-14) later in his letter telling these very same people how wonderfully gifted they are for service to God.

[4] Adams, pp. 80-81.

Since polygamy is frowned upon in our western society, this view has great appeal to modern Bible teachers, especially to those who do not want to put the study into it that Dr. Adams has done. However, as with the other views, there are at least a couple of objections.

The most obvious is that God instituted marriage to be monogamous for all people. Though some of His people did enter polygamous marriages, those marriages did not fulfill His intention for marriage. Since it was never God's plan anyway, it doesn't make sense for Paul to make a special case against it here. As we will see, that is not the most compelling argument against this teaching.

### Faithfulness to his wife

I believe this last view to be the best explanation of Paul's intent. As you have probably noticed throughout this study, I believe a literal interpretation is the first and best way to approach God's Word. Let's look at the phrase under consideration in its context regarding elders.

> [1]*It is a trustworthy statement: if any man aspires to the office of overseer, it is a fine work he desires to do.* [2]*An overseer, then, must be above reproach, the husband of one*

> *wife, temperate, prudent, respectable, hos-*
> *pitable, able to teach, [3]not addicted to wine*
> *or pugnacious, but gentle, peaceable, free*
> *from the love of money.*
>
> 1 Timothy 3:1-3

The previous two interpretations align our phrase with the marriage itself (divorce in the light of marriage and the number of partners in the marriage). However, this takes the phrase out of its immediate context. The surrounding phrases are referring to the *man*, not his relationships. The descriptions "above reproach", "temperate", "prudent", and "respectable" are all qualities, or characteristics, of the man. Remember that the literal translation is "one-woman man". "One-woman" cannot stand alone, like the other views attempt to make it do; it is an adjective describing the character of the man. A more expanded translation is that he is to be a "one-woman *type of* man". "One-woman" has nothing to do directly with the man's marriage or wife (or wives, past or present), but rather how he approaches his marriage.

Now it is true that the way he approaches marriage will indeed affect whether he is polygamous and if or how he divorces his wives, but those are just symptoms, visible results, of his character. Just like the other qualifications around it, "one-woman man" is a reference to the man's character in his marriage.

Some will argue that this is too simple and that all Christians are commanded in this way. While this is true, probably the most overlooked and ignored responsibility of church leaders (and especially elders) is that they are to be examples. Peter exhorted the elders to whom he wrote, "nor yet as lording [your divinely-appointed oversight] over those allotted to your charge, but proving to be examples to the flock" (1 Peter 5:3). Just as they are to be exemplary in all of the other character qualifications (which also apply to all Christians), those elders and deacons who are married should be the ideal examples of marital faithfulness before the flocks which they serve and all others around.

## A Final Thought

I should make one more point regarding elders and deacons before we close this section. I do not want any reader to get the impression that divorce is not a big deal to God. It is indeed. It is always caused by sin, and sin is a big deal. But divorce is *not*, like many churches seem to believe, the end of the road from which there is no hope of return. While a divorce or remarriage in itself does not automatically exclude a man from being considered for these positions, there may be other consequences of the divorce or remarriage that *may* disqualify him. Though I cannot give every possible situation here, allow me one example that will assist in explaining this final thought.

Imagine a man who, before he was saved, was well-known as a ladies' man. Not only did he flirt with every woman he met, but he was sexually active with other women as well. This lifestyle had led his wife to file for divorce. In time he was confronted with his sin and soon accepted Jesus Christ to be his Savior. Through attending church for a while he met a wonderful Christian woman; they dated and were finally married. Does his divorce eliminate him from being considered to be appointed as an elder or deacon? I do not think so. However, there may be some other things that do:

1. He, at this point, may not yet have a "good reputation with those outside the church" (1 Timothy 3:7).
2. He may also still not be considered "above reproach" (1 Timothy 3:2).
3. Depending on the period of time that has elapsed since his salvation, he may not have yet been "tested" (1 Timothy 3:10) and may still be considered a "new convert" (1 Timothy 3:6).

The divorce is not the issue here; it is the cause and consequences with which we must deal. Though he was forgiven for his sin at his salvation (as all Christians are when they repent), there are things that may cause him to never be a candidate for these positions. God may never allow his reputation to be unblemished among those with whom he formerly associated. He may never be considered "above reproach". These are all *consequences* of a life pattern of sin which can carry over into the Christian life. Only God's Spirit and a new life of extreme faithfulness, possibly over a long time, are able to make these effects fade away.

## "Widows Indeed"

In chapter nine we saw that Paul actually urged some widows to remarry. Others, however, he did not. Let's return to 1 Timothy 5 and look at two categories of widows according to Paul.

> ³Honor widows who are widows indeed; ⁴but if any widow has children or grandchildren, they must first learn to practice piety in regard to their own family and to make some return to their parents; for this is acceptable in the sight of God. ⁵Now she who is a widow indeed and who has been left alone, has fixed her hope on God and continues in entreaties and prayers night and day. ⁶But she who gives herself to wanton pleasure is dead even while she lives. ⁷Prescribe these things as well, so that they may be above reproach. ⁸But if anyone does not provide for his own, and especially for those of his household, he has denied the faith and is worse than an unbeliever.
>
> ⁹A widow is to be put on the list only if she is not less than sixty years old, having been the wife of one man, ¹⁰having a reputation for good works; and if she has brought up children, if she has shown hospitality to strangers, if she has washed the saints' feet, if she has assisted those in distress, and if she has devoted herself to every good work. ¹¹But refuse to put younger widows on the list, for when they feel sensual desires in disregard of Christ, they want to get married, ¹²thus incurring condemnation,

*because they have set aside their previous pledge. [13]At the same time they also learn to be idle, as they go around from house to house; and not merely idle, but also gossips and busybodies, talking about things not proper to mention. [14]Therefore, I want younger widows to get married, bear children, keep house, and give the enemy no occasion for reproach; [15]for some have already turned aside to follow Satan. [16]If any woman who is a believer has dependent widows, she must assist them and the church must not be burdened, so that it may assist those who are widows indeed.*

1 Timothy 5:3-16

I have already mentioned "widows indeed" in chapter nine. These godly women seem to be a special group of women who served the church in a unique way. In the following chart, look at a few of the similarities in the qualifications for elders, deacons, and these widows.

| **Elders** | **Deacons** | **Widows** |
| --- | --- | --- |
| *1 Timothy 3:1-7* | *1 Timothy 3:8-13* | *1 Timothy 5:10* |
| "must have a good reputation" (vs. 7) | "must also first be tested" (vs. 10) | "having a reputation for good works" |
| "manages his own household well…keeping his children under control" (vs. 4) | "good managers of *their* children and their own households" (vs. 12) | "brought up children" |
| "hospitable" (vs. 2) | | "shown hospitality to strangers" |

This is obviously not an exhaustive list, but rather just a few examples. Some people see a parallel in the middle of the list of deacon qualifications, where Paul adds,

> *Women must likewise be dignified, not malicious gossips, but temperate, faithful in all things.*
>
> 1 Timothy 3:11

There are two points about these special ministers that I would like to make. The first is about the phrase in 1 Timothy 5:9, "the wife of one man". If you remember the previous section on elders and deacons, this phrase should sound familiar. The reason is that it is the exact opposite of "the husband of one wife". Just as elders and deacons are to be "one-woman men", these widows are to be "one-man women". Since these women are required to have been widowed, they should have been examples of marital faithfulness for women as the elders and deacons are for men.

We do find one qualification for these widows regarding marriage that never appears for the others.

> [11]*But refuse to put younger widows on the list, for when they feel sensual desires in disregard of Christ, they want to get married,* [12]*thus incurring condemnation, because they have set aside their previous pledge.*

> 1 Timothy 5:11-12 [italics original]

Paul warned Timothy to put only certain widows "on the list", an obvious reference to the list of widows-indeed. As I stated in chapter nine, one of Paul's concerns was that younger widows would want to

165

remarry because of their sexual desires. Doing so would cause them to "set aside their previous pledge". It is possible that an additional requirement for widows-indeed was that they would pledge the remainder of their lives to service in the church, never to remarry. This restriction is not placed upon elders or deacons or even other women, but seems to be very possible for widows-indeed. One reason may be because of the age requirement – which is also never mentioned for the others – that widows-indeed were required to be *"not less than sixty years old"* (vs. 9).

The last point about this group of faithful servants concerns their income. The immediate context of 1 Timothy 5 is about providing for one's family. One of the qualifications of a widow-indeed was that she had no more family to support her. At sixty or older (well before our age of advanced medicine), she was probably unable to support herself. With no family, she would be left destitute. This is the point at which the church stepped in to help. It seems that these widows were to be given compensation for using their remaining years in special service in the church.

There are a couple of things that make this clear to me. First is the context of provision and support. The second comes from the original word translated "honor" in verse three. Paul used this very same word just a few verses down when he wrote,

> [17]*The elders who rule well are to be considered worthy of double* **honor**, *especially those who work hard at preaching and teaching.* [18]*For the Scripture says, "*YOU SHALL NOT MUZZLE THE OX WHILE HE IS THRESHING,*" and "The laborer is worthy of his wages."*
>
> 1 Timothy 5:17-18 [emphasis added]

In this case even the English makes it clear that financial remuneration is intended. However, a look at the Greek text gives us an added benefit. The word translated "honor" in both of these verses refers to money that is paid in compensation.[5] This "honor" that is to be given to elders and widows-indeed is monetary compensation for services rendered.

---

[5] BDAG, *time*.

## Other Positions

We have established that, while a divorced and/or remarried man cannot be automatically excluded from being considered for the positions of elder and deacon, there may be other consequences which do. Are there places for these Christians to serve? Of course! Remember the Corinthians? Paul told these people with extremely sordid pasts that they had been "washed...sanctified...[and] justified" (1 Corinthians 6:9-11). Not only that, but just six chapters later, Paul said that "each one [was] given the manifestation of the Spirit for the common good" (1 Corinthians 12:7). In the context of the chapter, this "manifestation of the Spirit" is obviously spiritual gifts for the specific use of service in the Body of Christ.

Unlike the offices of elder and deacon and the status of widow-indeed, the Bible does not make mention about any other "official" position with special qualifications. Every time God did not want something done because it was wrong, He specifically condemned that particular action. He did not condemn a divorced person for serving in the local church. In fact, other than those discussed above, He did not make any distinction between Christians who were single, married, divorced, or remarried, regarding how they are to serve in the local assembly. This would seem to make it clear that there should not be a problem with divorced people serving in His church. In fact, prohibiting these Christians to serve is in direct opposition for God's plan for their lives and the life of your local church.

# APPENDIX
## FIRST CORINTHIANS 7 EXAMINED

The purpose of this appendix is to answer the two questions that frequently arise regarding this chapter: *Is it really inspired?* and *Why does Paul seem to be against marriage?* Because of statements that Paul makes throughout this part of his letter, some people will attempt to discourage any use of this chapter in the doctrine of marriage, divorce, and remarriage. In the following sections, I will explain why we can not only rely on the teaching in this chapter but also gain necessary doctrine from it.

## Its Inspiration

> [10]*But to the married I give instructions, not I, but the Lord, that...*[12]*But to the rest I say, not the Lord, that...*
>
> 1 Corinthians 7:10, 12

Many people have a problem with these two verses because it sounds like Paul is giving some information from God (inspired – "not I, but the Lord") and some information from his own opinion (non-inspired - , "I say, not the Lord"). If we take 2 Timothy 3:16 to be true that "all Scripture is inspired by God", then we eliminate that from being a problem. However, it does bring up a valid question: what does Paul mean by these two phrases? There seems to be only one explanation that supports both the inerrancy of God's Word and the literal words that Paul used. Fortunately, my understanding does not contradict those scholars whom I respect and admire, so I confidently let them speak to this issue. All italics and bold print are from the original authors.

> This *I command*, says the apostle; *yet not I, but the Lord.* Not that he commanded any thing of his own head, or upon his own authority. Whatever he commanded was the Lord's command, dictated by his Spirit and enjoined by his authority. But his meaning is that the Lord himself, with his own mouth, had forbidden such separations, Mt. 5:32; 19:9; Mk. 10:11; Lu. 16:18... *But to the rest*

*speak I, not the Lord;* that is, the Lord had not so expressly spoken to this case as to the former divorce. It does not mean that the apostle spoke without authority from the Lord, or decided this case by his own wisdom, without the inspiration of the Holy Ghost. He closes this subject with a declaration to the contrary (v. 40), I think *also that I have the Spirit of God.*[1]

### Not I, but the Lord

Referring to Christ's declarations respecting divorce, Matthew 5:31, 32; 19:3-12. Not a distinction between an inspired and an uninspired saying. Paul means that his readers had no need to apply to him for instruction in the matter of divorce, since they had the words of Christ himself.

### I, not the Lord

These cases are not included in Christ's declarations.[2]

---

[1] Henry, p. 2255.

[2] Marvin Vincent, *Word Studies in the New Testament* (Grand Rapids: Eerdmans), vol.3, p. 218.

**Not I, but the Lord**. Paul had no commands from Jesus to the unmarried (men or women), but Jesus had spoken to the married (husbands and wives) as in Matthew 5:31f.; 19:3-12; Mark 10:9-12; Luke 16:18. The Master had spoken plain words about divorce. Paul reinforces his own inspired command by the command of Jesus. In Mark 10:9 we have from Christ: "What therefore God joined together let not man put asunder".

**But to the rest say I, not the Lord**. Paul has no word about marriage from Jesus beyond the problem of divorce. This is no disclaimer of inspiration. He simply means that here he is not quoting a command of Jesus.[3]

That's enough. I'm sure you get the point. No serious Bible student honestly believes that Paul's uninspired and error-prone opinion slipped into the Bible unnoticed. The overwhelming majority believe the same as those commentators quoted above: Jesus spoke to the first scenario, so Paul simply repeated Jesus' teaching. Since the second scenario had not yet arisen, Paul had nothing to fall back on.

---

[3] A.T. Robertson, *Word Pictures in the New Testament*, electronic edition, "1 Corinthians 7:10, 12".

However, his teaching was still inspired by God for the Corinthians then and for us today.

## Its Interpretation

The second complaint about this chapter is that, since Paul seems to really discourage marriage, some people do not understand how we can justify getting so much of our teaching from here. To understand the complaint, we have to examine the verses which contain the "problem".

> *6But this I say by way of concession, not of command. 7Yet **I wish that all men were even as I myself am**. However, each man has his own gift from God, one in this manner, and another in that.*

> *8But **I say to the unmarried** and to widows that **it is good for them if they remain even as I**...*

> *25Now concerning virgins I have no command of the Lord, but I give an opinion as one who by the mercy of the Lord is trustworthy. 26I think then that this is good in view of the present distress, that **it is good for a man to remain as he is**...29But this I say, brethren, the time has been shortened, so that from now on **those who have wives should be as though they had none**...*

> *39A wife is bound as long as her husband lives; but if her husband is dead, she is free to be married to whom she wishes,*

> *only in the Lord.* *40But **in my opinion she is happier if she remains as she is;** and I think that I also have the Spirit of God.*
>
> 1 Corinthians 7:6-8, 25-26, 29, 39-40
> [emphasis added]

I have taken the liberty of using bold print to emphasize the statements that seem to cause the problem. In reading this entire chapter, rather than focusing only on the parts in question, I believe that God, in His ever-wise way, gave us two explanations for Paul's attitude toward marriage.

## Marriage and Christian Service

The first reason Paul seems to be down on marriage is based on his own experience in Christ's service. This is found in verses 32 through 35:

> *32But I want you to be free from concern. One who is unmarried is concerned about the things of the Lord, how he may please the Lord; 33but one who is married is concerned about the things of the world, how he may please his wife, 34and his interests are divided. The woman who is unmarried, and the virgin, is concerned about the things of the Lord, that she may be holy both in body*

*and spirit; but one who is married is con-
cerned about the things of the world, how
she may please her husband. [35]This I say for
your own benefit; not to put a restraint
upon you, but to promote what is appropri-
ate and to secure undistracted devotion to
the Lord.*

Many Bible scholars believe that Paul may have been married earlier in life. While we cannot be certain on this point, we do know that he was unmarried during every recorded part of his life. His wish and encouragement that Christians would be like him (vs. 7-8) was because he knew that married life can negatively affect the amount of time and effort that a Christian will put into the ministry. This is easily seen in the teaching that a Christian's priorities should be God, family, and ministry, in that order. Whether that is how God desires our priorities to be or not, Paul knew that it is how we humans are. So he said, "If you are able to withstand the sexual temptation that will go along with remaining single, *do it!* Your service will be much more effective without the pressures of marriage and home life."

## *The Cultural Circumstances*

The other explanation for Paul's discouragement of marriage had to do with the time period in which he wrote. Look at how he described his situation:

> 26*I think then that this is good in view of **the present distress**, that it is good for a man to remain as he is...*28*But if you marry, you have not sinned; and if a virgin marries, she has not sinned. Yet such will have **trouble in this life**, and I am trying to spare you.* 29*But this I say, brethren, **the time has been shortened**...*[31]*for **the form of this world is passing away**.*

1 Corinthians 7:26, 28-29, 31b
[emphasis added]

In order to grasp the intensity of what Paul called "the present distress", we have to understand a little about the time during which he wrote. It is generally accepted that Paul wrote this letter to the Corinthians about A.D. 56. A look at any trustworthy history book informs us that from A.D. 54-68 the emperor of Rome was the diabolical Nero. For those who may know nothing of this man, read these descriptions:

> A greater contrast can hardly be imagined than that between Paul, one of

the purest and noblest of men, and Nero, one of the basest and vilest of tyrants. The glorious first five years of Nero's reign (54-59) under the wise guidance of Seneca and Burrhus, make the other nine (59-68) only more hideous by contrast. We read his life with mingled feelings of contempt for his folly, and horror of his wickedness. The world was to him a comedy and a tragedy, in which he was to be the chief actor. He had an insane passion for popular applause; he played on the lyre; he sung his odes at supper; he drove his chariots in the circus; he appeared as a mimic on the stage, and compelled men of the highest rank to represent in dramas or in [shows] the obscenest of the Greek myths. But the comedian was surpassed by the tragedian. He heaped crime upon crime until he became a proverbial monster of iniquity. The murder of his brother (Britannicus), his mother (Agrippina), his wives (Octavia and Poppaea), his teacher (Seneca), and many eminent Romans, was fitly followed by his suicide in the thirty-second year of his age. With him the family of Julius Caesar ignominiously perished, and the empire became the prize of successful soldiers and adventurers.[4]

---

[4] Philip Schaff, ed., *History of the Christian Church*, electronic edition, §37.

Nero ranks with Gaius for folly and vice, while his cruelties recall the worst years of Tiberius. Very effeminate in his tastes, particular about the arrangement of his hair and proud of his voice, his greatest fault was inordinate vanity which courted applause for performances on non-Roman lines. He neglected his high office and degraded Roman *gravitas* by zeal for secondary pursuits. Nero, like his three predecessors, was very susceptible to female charms. He was licentious in the extreme, even to guilt of that nameless vice of antiquity—love of a male favorite. His cruelty, both directly and through his instruments, made the latter part of his reign as detestable as the [first five years] had been golden. He loved the extravagant and luxurious in every exaggerated form. He was a weakling and a coward in his life, and especially in his death. Of his personal appearance we are told his features were regular and good; the expression of his countenance, however, was somewhat repelling. His frame was ill proportioned—slender legs and big stomach. In later years his face was covered with pimples.[5]

---

[5] James Orr, ed. *International Standard Bible Encyclopedia*, electronic edition, "Nero".

Second only to Domitian (who ruled Rome A.D. 81-96), Nero was the most cruel of the Roman emperors in the acting out of his hatred toward Christians. Tradition says that Nero would use live Christians as torches to illuminate his famous gardens.

These were the circumstances in which Paul and his readers (most of whom were Gentile and possibly Roman citizens) lived. Because of the sporadic outbursts of Nero's insane persecution of Christians, it is no wonder that Paul discouraged marriage in favor of unceasing Christian evangelism and ministry. It is obvious in 1 Thessalonians 4:13-18 (written around A.D. 51) that Paul believed he would live to see Jesus return. His statements like "the time has been shortened" and "the form of this world is passing away" show us that he undoubtedly believed that they were living in the final days before Christ's return.

Paul's intent in making these statements was obviously not to call marriage bad. In fact, multiple times he said that for his readers to marry would *not* be bad or sin (vs. 9, 28, 36). So there is no contradiction between his teaching on marriage, divorce, and remarriage and his parent-like concerns for his immediate readers.

# SCRIPTURE INDEX

8oz Sr cream ⎤ 35U
                for
1/4 C mayo ⎦ 25
              m
garlic powder
S + P
1 can artichoke
        & s
1 C frozen spinach
  1/4 C moz + pam

CPSIA information can be obtained
at www.ICGtesting.com
Printed in the USA
FFOW04n0531041016
28187FF